Lý Quí Phát,
the father of my mothers

Lê Kiêm Gương,
the mother of my mothers

With my mother and the rambutans

SECRETS
from My
VIETNAMESE
KITCHEN

KIM THÚY

SECRETS
from My
VIETNAMESE
KITCHEN

Simple Recipes from My Many Mothers

Translated from the French by Sheila Fischman
Recipes translated by Marie Asselin

appetite
by RANDOM HOUSE

Published by arrangement with Groupe Librex, Montréal, Québec, Canada

Appetite by Random House® and colophon are registered trademarks of Penguin Random House LLC.

Library and Archives of Canada Cataloguing in Publication is available upon request.
ISBN: 9780525610229
eBook ISBN: 9780525610236

Book design: adapted from a design by Marike Paradis
Cover and book photography: Sarah Scott, www.sarahscottphoto.ca
Photos of Kim Thúy's family and food photography: Sarah Scott
Photos of Vietnam: Gilles Dufour
Photos on pages 150 and 160: Andy Long Hoang
Photos on pages 138 and 166 and 167: Trí Nguyen
Photo on page 174: Quốc Lý
Printed and bound in China

Published in Canada by Appetite by Random House®,
a division of Penguin Random House Canada Limited.

www.penguinrandomhouse.ca

10   9   8   7   6   5   4   3   2   1

I couldn't possibly count the number of meals I have cooked for my husband, Francis, and our sons, Justin and Valmond. My kitchen opens at 3 p.m., when Valmond comes home from school. As soon as he's in the doorway, I switch on the stove. "Pasta or rice?" As if I were running a restaurant, he chooses: "Chicken? Fish? Pork?"

Around five o'clock, I start making my second meal. Justin has never eaten from the kids' menu, whether at home or not. We've always shared with him whatever we eat. He has no allergies, so he eats everything, unlike Valmond, who is autistic and has as many strictures about how food must be cooked as he has about spices and ingredients. Justin loves everything, from the gizzards in *salade aux gésiers* to shepherd's pie or Thai curried tofu, mussels, carpaccio . . . Once, when he was around ten, Justin was offended by a waiter who expressed doubt when he ordered sweetbreads from the menu. So that's why I always prepare a different dish for Justin, so as not to impose Valmond's constraints on him.

My last service is for Francis, around seven-thirty or eight o'clock. Even when we're just having spaghetti, I cook a new batch because it wouldn't taste as good if it were heated up in the microwave or even on the stove. It goes without saying that a dish of sautéed vegetables must be eaten right away, and it's the same for a saddle of lamb. I light up the stove burner again, which rarely has had enough time to cool down.

From 3 p.m. to 9 p.m., Valmond has a thousand small requests: fresh corn sliced from the cob, cookies, bagel with cream cheese, buttered naan, freshly squeezed lime juice, and so on.

This means that there's nearly as much activity in my home kitchen as in the one in my former restaurant. My routine may seem demanding, but I must confess that I have two reasons for doing it. The first has to do with how I am unable to verbalize my love for my family or even display it with affectionate gestures. Like my parents and my large Vietnamese family, I depend on food to express as best I can my unconditional love for them all. The second reason: I firmly believe that to make a person happy or to know what it is that brings pleasure is a privilege to be cherished. Cooking allows me to use that privilege nearly every day, three times an evening, and in that way, to experience a daily type of bliss.

CONTENTS

INTRODUCTION

The moment you step inside a Vietnamese house,
you are bombarded with variations on a single greeting:
"Have you eaten?" "What would you like to eat?"
"Come and eat." "Just one little bite." "The chicken
I cooked is still hot." "Here, try my cream puffs."

We are not in the habit of verbalizing our joys, or even less, our affection. We use food as a tool for expressing our emotions. My parents don't say, "We've missed you," but rather, "We've made some spring rolls," knowing that I love to eat them anytime, anywhere. Similarly, when I'm traveling abroad on a book tour, they will report that my sons had three helpings of everything, as a way to reassure me. On our visits to my grandmother in New York, my mother would stuff the trunk with her own mother's favorite dishes. My father would laugh at her, but he still flies to Washington, D.C., and loads Vietnamese dishes into the trunk of the car that will take him to my uncle's house in a remote part of Pennsylvania. That ninety-two-year-old uncle is my father's older brother, who fed and housed him during my father's time at university. My father considers him a father figure, and he tries to express his gratitude through the best sausage, the best lemongrass beef stew, the best steamed pancakes, the best sticky rice cake, and the best dried shrimp to be found in the Vietnamese markets.

1

In the refugee camps, my mother and Aunts 6 and 8 would do their best to transform the fish rations we'd receive six days out of seven in an effort to bring a semblance of normality to mealtimes. One day my mother was able to make a thin dough for dumplings. I remember very clearly how she was sitting on the ground with the cover of the barrel that we used as a water tank. She rolled out her dough on that rusty metal plate, which here and there still bore spots of its original yellow paint. The meal that followed was almost beside the point—we were just thrilled to see her cooking something other than rice and fish. It was a moment of togetherness, of celebration.

Recently someone asked me to describe my most memorable meal. It's impossible for me to make a list of all the culinary experiences I've been lucky enough to enjoy. Some stood out just as much for the conviviality around the table as for the food produced by talented chefs. How to choose among them all? There was an evening when we laughed until we cried over a huge platter of oysters and a meal in which the master sushi chef ensured that it was a matter of mere seconds between when he placed the piece of fish on the ball of rice and when we tasted it. But then how could I not mention the perogies made by my Polish editor's mother, or the irreplaceable meal of Vietnamese clams, or the slice of pear and pistachio pie eaten on the steps of a church? How not to mention the fresh pasta in a restaurant with a glass roof in the middle of a park in Palermo? And what about Francis's unsurpassable lobster sandwich? Add to all of these the grand receptions I have attended, such as the ones hosted by the king of Malaysia and Princess Caroline of Hanover, the prime ministers, government ministers and ambassadors . . .

Having said that, of all those feasts and the everyday dishes I've eaten, a single meal is engraved in my memory, in my heart, on my being:

Before plastic glasses were in use all over the planet, merchants in Southeast Asia sold drinks by emptying a bottle into a transparent plastic bag filled with ice. They would then insert a straw and close the bag with an elastic.

This enabled them to keep the bottle so it could be returned. I don't know by what miracle we came into possession of a bag filled with a soft drink during our time in the refugee camp. There were thirteen of us gathered around that bag in the blazing sun. We hadn't had truly drinkable water, nor had we been in contact with anything cold, for months. Drops of condensation sparkled in the heat like precious diamonds. We passed the bag from hand to hand, starting with my youngest brother, Nhơn, who was barely six years old. I was sure that the little bag would go around the circle only one time because we were all so thirsty, yet we made it last three tours. Without having to say anything, we all held back and only wet our lips each time it was our turn.

Along with the thousand invaluable lessons I learned from that experience, it confirmed to me that I was raised by a village and raised up by the strength and dignity of the members of that village. It's thanks to them that I became the human I am today.

On the following pages, you will meet my mother and my aunt-mothers. In South Vietnam, we often identify ourselves by the number that represents our birth order in the family. As the number one is reserved for the most important person in a village, we start counting at two. My mother is the second child in her family, which is why her younger sisters call her Big Sister 3 and I call my aunts by their number: Aunts 4, 5, 6, 7, and 8. In this way, the hierarchy and authority are always present during conversations and when we refer to one another.

BIG SISTER 3 — *LÝ KIM THỦY*

My mother is very good at math. Had she been born at another time, in another environment, she would have tried to become an engineer.

As it was, she very easily obtained a degree in aeronautical technology during our first years in Canada. I think she would have been an excellent teacher because she loves passing on what she knows. She often tells us that she takes us from one shore to the other like a ferry. I would say that she is more like a Sherpa, guiding us in our travels.

5

THE FUNDAMENTALS

Bún

Bánh hỏi

Hù tiếu

Bún tàu

Bún gạo

Bánh phở

RICE NOODLES

*Just as Italians have many varieties of pasta,
the Vietnamese have a specific kind of rice noodle for every dish.*

Vietnamese soup is made with flat noodles. Some people prefer the broad ones while others choose medium width, but in any case, they must be flat. Imperial rolls are served with round rice noodles. The highly seasoned meal-size beef soup from Huê calls for round, thick rice noodles, while lemongrass beef stew just somehow tastes better with a flat one. Choosing the wrong size or shape of noodle to serve will result in at best a shower of commentary, at worst an attack on the whole family tree!

Unlike Italian pasta, rice noodles are exceptionally fragile. The most sensible and easy way to cook them successfully is to submerge them in a pot of cold water and heat them on the stove. As soon as the water boils, turn off the heat. Depending on the size of the noodles, leave them for three to seven minutes to obtain the desired consistency. Drain, then rinse with cold water. This method will allow you to serve up perfect rice noodles and preserve the honor of the entire family!

Vietnamese coriander

Paddy herbs

Betel leaves

Long coriander

Mint

Thai basil

Garlic chives

Cilantro

Fish mint

HERBS

Vietnamese cuisine could almost be defined by the scents and aromas of fresh herbs. If I had to choose one word to describe our food, I would say "freshness." Even when we make a piquant and highly seasoned dish, the peppers are often added or served fresh: whole, chopped, or thinly sliced.

Whether it is a Vietnamese soup or a skewer of grilled meat, fresh herbs are served with nearly all dishes. We eat them raw, with no vinaigrette, salt, or oil. A soup of field crabs and tomatoes always comes with a plate of banana flowers, water spinach, and shiso. A gently simmered stew of fish and eggplant is defined by the accompanying basket of water-lily stems, bean sprouts, and a mixture of herbs. As for fish with turmeric, it contains three times as much dill as fish. And you must have winged beans on the side to fully express the taste of shrimp cooked in their own eggs.

When I had my restaurant Ru de Nam, at the end of the day I couldn't eat anything I'd cooked except for spring rolls. I never tire of them because of their particular amalgamation of herbs: fish mint, garlic chives, Thai basil, Vietnamese coriander, mint, coriander. Their freshness is released with the very first bite. Their aromas merge and change as they are chewed. In the throat, they leave a memory of their perfume long afterward . . . like a lover's kiss.

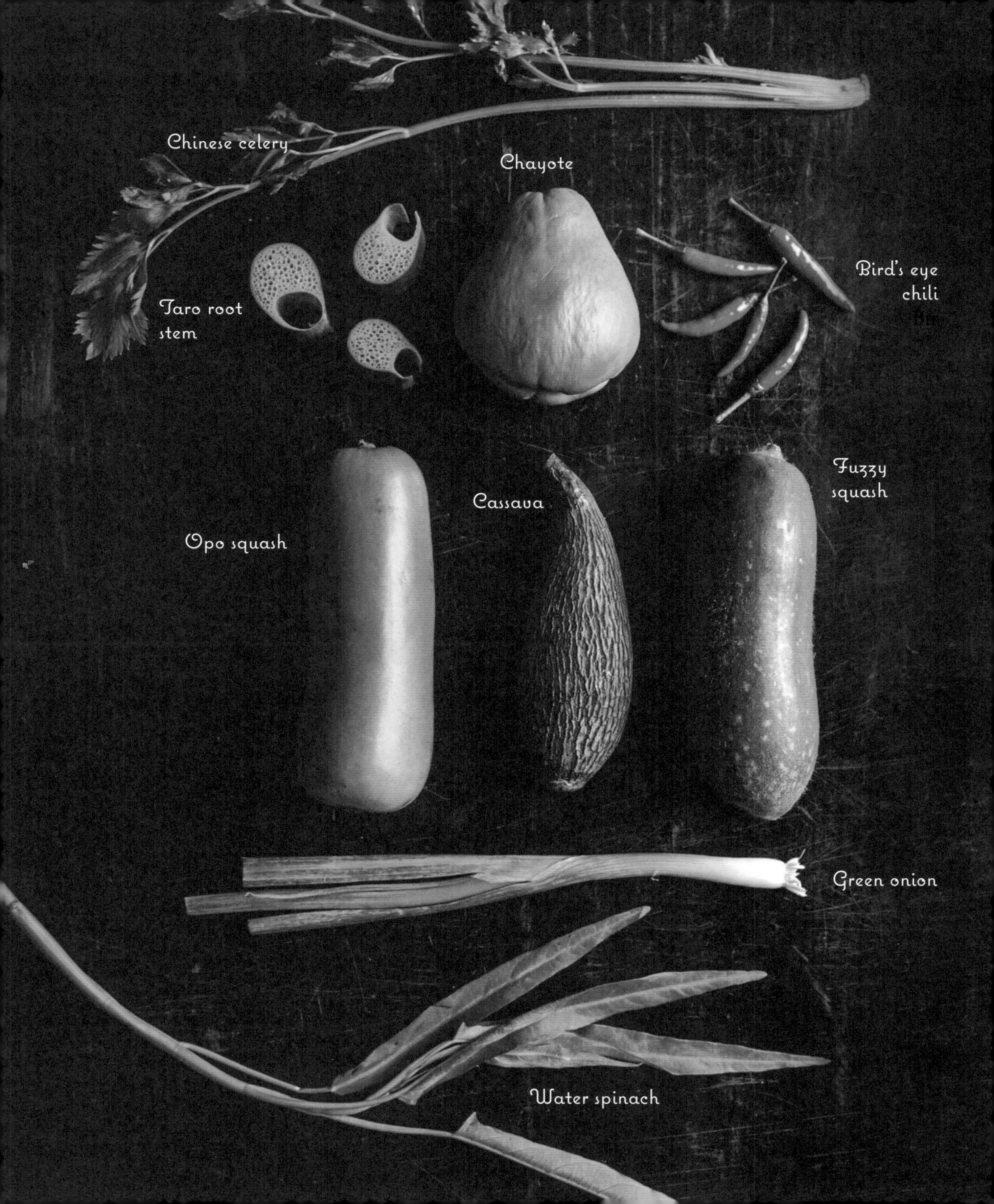

Chinese celery

Chayote

Taro root
stem

Bird's eye
chili

Fuzzy
squash

Opo squash

Cassava

Green onion

Water spinach

VEGETABLES

At mealtimes, all the dishes are put on the table together, to be shared. There's no order. We can take a bite of meat, then a spoonful of soup, followed by a piece of fish, then another sip of soup. The courteous hostess might turn her chopsticks around to use the clean ends to place the choicest morsel in the rice bowl of a guest. There's always a lot of to-ing and fro-ing around the dishes.

The platter of vegetables is generally the most voluminous of all. It may be piled high with water spinach or sautéed chayote, okra, or blanched cabbage. Vegetables, raw or cooked, play the main role, while meat is content to be in the chorus. That explains why, during one of the first times I was invited to eat supper with a local family in Granby, when we were still new to Canada, I spontaneously took the piece of steak placed on my plate and moved it to the middle of the table, thinking that it was meant to be shared among everyone. Beside that enormous serving of meat, the few slices of carrot looked like a decoration.

Our family's eating habits are very different now after forty years in Quebec. Servings of meat are more copious, but the platter of vegetables hasn't changed. We determine portions of asparagus not by the number of spears, but in terms of a half-bunch per person. Bok choy comes in 18-ounce bags, and daikon are the size of baseball bats.

In short, if a Vietnamese person designed a fridge, one drawer would be reserved for meat, and the rest for vegetables.

Papaya

Love apple

Sugar apple

Longan

Jackfruit

FRUIT

South Vietnam has a sweet tooth for delicacies of all kinds: thin strips of candied coconut, dried jackfruits, freshly squeezed sugarcane juice, tapioca pudding, cassava cake, cashew and sesame-seed squares, caramel flan, fried bananas, red-bean ice cream . . . These treats are eaten at any hour of the day.

During the 1990s, when I was a lawyer in Hanoi, at the end of the day I would go out for two or three small balls of sticky rice stuffed with mung beans. I'd enjoy my treat while sitting on a small plastic stool just inches from the ground on a bit of sidewalk.

At the end of a meal, we generally serve a plate of several pieces of fruit, peeled and sliced, that "line the inside of the mouth with a new taste," which is the literal meaning of our term for dessert, *tráng miệng*. Unlike apples and pears, fruits like durians, pineapples, sapotes, mangosteens, rambutans, pomelos, longans, mangoes, and papayas require some effort from us before they give us their flesh. These fruits offer the intoxicating tastes of the sun and the scents of tropical heat. They are so essential, such an obvious part of everyday life in Vietnam, that plates of fruit very comfortably sit next to the large bottles of cognac and the array of imported beers in karaoke bars.

For the Vietnamese, fruit is king!

RICE PAPER

Forty years ago, rice paper wrappers were hard to find in our town of Granby. My mother tried making them at home, but it was not a total success—actually, it was mostly a failure.

Nowadays, they're easy to find in great variety: large, small, square, round. Dry, they're very brittle, but rehydrated, they become pliant and as soft as a baby's skin. They don't tolerate a second rehydration, however, so they must be used before they dry again. For that reason, it's a good idea to place spray bottles filled with warm water on the table. Each person can then moisten the rice paper at the moment it's needed to make a roll.

If rice paper refuses to soften after thirty seconds of hydration, it probably never will. The best solution is to discard it and start again with a new one.

BARRELS OF FISH SAUCE

Most Vietnamese couldn't cook, couldn't EXIST, without fish sauce, a preparation of anchovies fermented in salt for twelve months. Don't be put off by the odor. The taste is nothing like the smell. Be advised, though, that if you start to use it, you will always want it, since no other ingredient has its unique taste.

My Uncle 9 will tell you that a rare steak will never be as good as when the taste is intensified by a few drops of fish sauce with fresh hot chili pepper just a moment before you bite into it. And I'm with him completely—black peppercorn (hot) sauce comes nowhere near it. Perhaps it's a matter of taste or a childhood memory, but we consider ourselves to be totally impartial on this crucial matter!

One day when we were deep inside the darkness of a cube van on our way to pick strawberries or beans, my mother told me about a woman, a day laborer, who would wait for her employer across from my maternal grandfather's place every morning. And every morning my grandfather's gardener brought her a portion of sticky rice wrapped in a banana leaf. Every morning, standing in the truck that was taking her to the rubber trees, she watched the gardener move away in the middle of the bougainvillea garden. One morning she didn't see him cross the dirt road to bring her breakfast. Then another morning . . . and another. One night she gave my mother a sheet of paper darkened with question marks, nothing else. My mother never saw her again in the truck jam-packed with workers. That young girl never went back to the plantations or to the bougainvillea garden. She disappeared not knowing that the gardener had asked his parents in vain for permission to marry her. No one told her that my grandfather had accepted the request of the gardener's parents to send him to another town. No one told her that the gardener, her own love, had been forced to go away, unable to leave her a letter because she was illiterate, because she was a young woman traveling in the company of men, because her skin had been burned too dark by the sun.

—from the novel *Ru* by Kim Thúy

21

DIPPING FISH SAUCE
— NƯỚC MẮM CHUA

Makes 1 cup (250 mL) ✦ Prep time 5 minutes

¼ cup (50 g) sugar
½ cup (125 mL) water
¼ cup (60 mL) fish sauce

¼ cup (60 mL) lime juice, rice vinegar,
    or white vinegar

1—Add all ingredients to a bowl and stir until the sugar is fully dissolved.

Store in an airtight container for up to 1 month in the refrigerator.

FISH SAUCE DRESSING
— NƯỚC MẮM GỎI

Makes about 1¾ cups (430 mL) ✦ Prep time 5 minutes

½ cup (100 g) sugar
½ cup (125 mL) water
½ cup (125 mL) fish sauce

½ cup (125 mL) lime juice, rice vinegar,
    or white vinegar

1—Add all ingredients to a bowl and stir until the sugar is fully dissolved.

The ingredients for this dressing are exactly the same as for the dipping fish sauce. The only difference is the decreased ratio of water to the other elements, which produces a more concentrated flavor. Store in an airtight container for up to 1 month in the refrigerator.

GREEN ONION SAUCE
— MỞ HÀNH

Makes about 1¼ cups (310 mL) ✦ Prep time 15 minutes ✦ Cook time 15 minutes

1 cup (250 mL) vegetable oil

12 to 15 green onions, white and green parts, sliced into rounds

1—Add oil to a large stainless-steel skillet and place over medium-high heat. 2—Add the green onions and stir until they start sizzling, then remove from heat. 3—Let stand for 10 minutes, stirring from time to time.

Store in an airtight container for up to 1 month in the refrigerator.

Back in Saigon, we used to render small cubes of lard in this sauce, which added flavor to the oil and would fry up into crispy snacks, similar to pork rinds.

FLAVORED HOISIN SAUCE
— *TƯƠNG*

Makes 1⅔ cups (400 mL) ✦ Prep time 10 minutes ✦ Cook time 5 minutes

1 cup (250 mL) water, divided
1 Tbsp (9 g) glutinous rice flour or cornstarch
½ cup (125 mL) hoisin sauce

2 Tbsp (30 mL) soy sauce
Chili paste or fresh bird's eye chilies, to taste
Crushed peanuts

1—Pour half of the water into a small bowl, then whisk in the rice flour. Set aside.
2—To a small saucepan set over medium heat, add the remaining water, hoisin sauce, and soy sauce, and stir until well blended. 3—Whisk in the reserved flour and water mixture, bring to a boil, and simmer until the mixture becomes sticky. Remove from heat. 4—Season with chili paste and sprinkle with crushed peanuts.

Serve hot, warm, or cold.

Some people use peanut butter to thicken this sauce. I personally prefer the crunch of crushed peanuts.

TOASTED RICE FLOUR
— THÍNH

Makes ½ cup (125 mL) ✦ Prep time 5 minutes + resting ✦ Cook time 15 minutes

⅔ cup (185 g) long-grain white rice or glutinous rice

1—In a stainless-steel skillet over medium heat, dry-roast the rice until the grains have changed color and are well toasted, about 15 minutes. 2—Remove from heat and let cool completely, then use a food processor or blender to grind to a fine powder.

Store in an airtight container.

You can buy packaged toasted rice flour in Asian grocery stores, but making it yourself allows you to enjoy the delightful aroma of toasting rice. You can also toast rice in the oven; just place the rice on a baking sheet and toast at 300°F (150°C) for a few minutes, until golden. Try it sometime, even if you don't need the flour!

JASMINE RICE
— CƠM

Serves 2 ✤ Prep time 5 minutes ✤ Cook time 10 minutes + resting

1 cup (195 g) jasmine rice   1½ cups (375 mL) cold water

1—Put the rice in an 8-cup (2 L) saucepan, then add enough water to cover. Rub the rice between your fingers for a few seconds. 2—Drain the water and repeat the same process one or two times, until the water drains almost clear. Drain excess water. 3—Add the 1½ cups (375 mL) cold water to the saucepan with the rice and bring to a boil. 4—Lower the heat to very low, cover, and simmer for 10 minutes. 5—Remove from heat and let rest, covered, for 5 minutes. 6—Fluff the rice with a fork or chopsticks and serve immediately.

RICE COOKER METHOD

1—Put the rice in an 8-cup (2 L) saucepan and add enough water to cover. Rub the rice between your fingers for a few seconds. 2—Drain the water and repeat the same process one or two times, until the water drains almost clear. Drain thoroughly. 3—Transfer the rice to the container of a rice cooker. Add the 1½ cups (375 mL) cold water, put the lid on the rice cooker, and turn it on. 4—Once the cooking cycle is done, let the rice rest for 5 minutes. 5—Fluff the rice with a fork or chopsticks and serve immediately.

The traditional method to measure how much water you should add to different amounts of rice is to use your index finger, obviously! So, to be *extremely* precise, you add any amount of rice to your container, making sure it's evenly distributed. Place the tip of your index finger, pointing down, on the surface of the rice and then pour in water until it almost reaches the first joint of your finger.

VIETNAMESE PICKLED VEGETABLES
— ĐỒ CHUA

Makes 2 cups (500 mL) ✤ Prep time 10 minutes + resting and marinating

2 cups (500 mL) julienned vegetables
(carrots and/or daikon)
1 tsp (6 g) salt

¼ cup (60 mL) rice vinegar
2 Tbsp (25 g) sugar

1—In a bowl, combine the vegetables with the salt and let rest for 15 minutes. 2—Pat the vegetables dry. 3—Combine the rice vinegar and sugar in a 3-cup (750 mL) Mason jar. Add the vegetables, screw the lid on, and gently shake the jar to combine. 4—Leave to marinate in the refrigerator for at least 30 minutes, shaking the jar a few times during the process.

Store for up to 5 days in the refrigerator.

PICKLED SHALLOTS
— HÀNH CHUA

Makes 1 cup (250 mL) ✤ Prep time 10 minutes + marinating

1 cup (160 g) thinly sliced shallots (use a
mandoline if you have one)

½ cup (125 mL) rice vinegar
Salt

1—Place the sliced shallots in a 2-cup (500 mL) Mason jar. Add the rice vinegar, season with salt, screw the lid on, and gently shake the jar to combine. 2—Leave to marinate in the refrigerator for at least 15 minutes.

Store for up to 1 week in the refrigerator.

VERMICELLI, VEGETABLE, AND FRESH HERB PLATTER
— *RAU*

Serves 4 ✦ Prep time 15 minutes

4 large lettuce leaves

1½ cups (260 g) cooked and cooled rice
   vermicelli

1 to 2 cucumbers, cut into sticks

1 star fruit, sliced

1 large handful bean sprouts

5 to 6 sprigs (each) fresh cilantro, Thai basil,
   mint, Vietnamese coriander, shiso, fish mint

1—Arrange the lettuce leaves on a large serving plate and add the rice vermicelli, cucumber sticks, star fruit slices, and bean sprouts. Garnish with the fresh herbs.

This combination of herbs and vegetables is almost as essential to Vietnamese cuisine as rice. It is used in spring rolls and served with grilled meats. Some regions of Vietnam will add other varieties of vegetables and herbs to the mix. When you eat Vietnamese food, you'll often find yourself tasting ten flavors in one bite!

AUNT 4 — *LÝ KIM HÀ*

She waited for her husband for ten years.
For ten years, her husband longed for her.

Once a month she managed to make a reservation at the post office in Saigon to receive a fifteen-minute telephone call from her husband. As relations between the United States and Vietnam had broken off in the 1980s, he had to drive from Washington, D.C., to Montreal over the weekend to make that phone call. Twelve hours each way, for several years. Nowadays they delight in the happiness of their four sons and their five grandchildren, all living in Washington, D.C.

35

SOUPS

LIGHT BROTH, OR PALATE CLEANSER
— CANH

Serves 4 to 6 ✦ Prep time 5 minutes ✦ Cook time 5 minutes

6 cups (1.5 L) water

1½ Tbsp (22.5 mL) fish sauce

1½ cups (45 g) spinach or other leafy greens

1—Combine the water and fish sauce in a large saucepan and bring to a boil. 2—Add the spinach, stir to combine, and remove from heat. Serve immediately.

During a Vietnamese meal, all the dishes are served at once, set in the center of the dining table. We might start by eating a slice of pork, followed by a bite of vegetables and a piece of fish. We'll then have a sip of broth before returning to the meat. The order is the diner's choice.

BAMBOO SHOOT AND PORK SOUP
— CANH MĂNG

Serves 4 to 6 ✦ Prep time 25 minutes ✦ Cook time 1 hour 15 minutes

8 cups (2 L) water

3 Tbsp (45 mL) fish sauce

1 pork leg (knuckle and trotter),
   chopped into 2 to 3 pieces

1 can (227 mL) sliced bamboo shoots

1 bunch fresh cilantro, coarsely chopped

Green onions, white and green parts,
   sliced into rounds, to taste

1—Add the water and fish sauce to a stockpot, then add the pork leg. Bring to a boil, then lower the heat and cover. 2—Simmer for 1 hour, or until the meat is falling off the bone. 3—Remove the pork leg from the cooking liquid. Debone the meat, then separate the meat from the rind. 4—Discard the bones. Cut the rind into strips and shred the meat. Set the rind and the meat aside in separate dishes. If needed, add cold water to the pot to bring the quantity of liquid back to 8 cups (2 L). Skim the broth. 5—Rinse the bamboo shoots several times, then drain well and add to the broth. 6—Add the shredded meat and half of the rind. Bring back to a simmer and skim again. Simmer for 5 minutes. 7—Ladle into bowls, garnish with fresh cilantro and green onions, and serve.

Serve the soup piping hot and let everyone add more pork rind to their serving as they wish.

STUFFED SQUASH SOUP
— CANH BẦU

Serves 4 to 6 ✦ Prep time 20 minutes ✦ Cook time 45 minutes

½ lb (225 g) ground pork
½ lb (225 g) raw shrimp, peeled and
  coarsely chopped
½ cup (60 g) minced onions
2½ Tbsp (37.5 mL) fish sauce, divided
Freshly ground black pepper

2 to 3 Vietnamese squashes (opo or fuzzy),
  each about 3 inches (8 cm) in diameter,
  peeled
6 cups (1.5 L) water
2 green onions, white and green parts,
  sliced into thin rounds, divided
1 large handful fresh cilantro, coarsely
  chopped, divided

1—To a large stainless-steel bowl, add the pork, shrimp, minced onions, and 1 tablespoon (15 mL) of the fish sauce. Generously season with black pepper and, using your hands, mix until the ingredients are thoroughly combined. Set aside. 2—Slice the squashes into 4-inch (10 cm) pieces. Using a melon baller, hollow out the center of each piece to create tubes. 3—Stuff the squash tubes with the pork and shrimp mixture, pressing in firmly, then set the squash aside. 4—In a large stockpot, bring the water to a boil, then pour in the remaining fish sauce. 5—Remove the pot from heat and add the stuffed squash to the hot broth. 6—Put the pot back onto medium heat, return the broth to a simmer, and cook for 25 to 30 minutes or until the squash becomes translucent. 7—Add half of the green onions and cilantro, lower the heat to the minimum, cover, and keep cooking for 10 minutes. 8—Ladle the cooking broth into a serving bowl, then add the stuffed squash and garnish with the remaining green onions and cilantro. 9—Cut the stuffed squash into thick slices and allow diners to ladle the soup into individual bowls.

The longer you let the flavors infuse, the better the soup is. You can prepare it hours in advance and reheat it when you're ready to serve. (Garnish with reserved cilantro and green onions just before serving.) If you can't find opo or fuzzy squashes, you can substitute green, yellow, or white zucchini.

TOFU AND GARLIC CHIVE SOUP
— CANH ĐẬU HỦ & TIM GÀ

Serves 4 to 6 ✦ Prep time 10 minutes + resting ✦ Cook time 5 minutes

½ cup (70 g) chicken giblets (kidneys, hearts, gizzards), sliced into strips

2½ Tbsp (37.5 mL) fish sauce

Peanut oil, for cooking

1 cup (250 mL) halved straw mushrooms

1 cup (250 g) medium-firm tofu cut into ½-inch (1.2 cm) cubes

6 cups (1.5 L) water

1 cup (60 g) garlic chives cut into ½-inch (1.2 cm) lengths

Freshly ground black pepper

1—Place the giblets in a bowl. Add the fish sauce and let rest for 5 minutes. 2—Heat a splash of oil in a stockpot set over medium-high heat, then add the giblets and sauté for 1 minute. 3—Add the mushrooms and tofu and cook for 1 more minute. 4—Add the water and bring to a boil. Remove from heat, then stir in the chives. Season with black pepper and serve immediately.

MEATBALL AND CHRYSANTHEMUM GREENS SOUP
— CANH TẦN Ô

Serves 4 to 6 ✦ Prep time 20 minutes ✦ Cook time 10 minutes

¾ lb (340 g) ground pork

¼ lb (110 g) raw shrimp, peeled and
  coarsely chopped

½ cup (60 g) minced onions

¼ cup (60 mL) fish sauce, divided

Freshly ground black pepper

12 cups (3 L) water

2 large handfuls chrysanthemum greens

2 green onions, white and green parts,
  sliced into thin rounds

1—To a large stainless-steel bowl, add the pork, shrimp, minced onions, and 1 tablespoon (15 mL) of the fish sauce. Generously season with black pepper and, using your hands, mix until the ingredients are thoroughly combined. Set aside. 2—In a large pot, bring the water to a boil, then pour in the remaining fish sauce. 3—Using two small spoons, pick up about 2 teaspoons (10 mL) of the pork and shrimp mixture. Shape the mixture into a small meatball, then drop it into the boiling water. Repeat the steps until the whole surface of the water is crowded with meatballs. 4—Simmer for 5 minutes, then add the chrysanthemum greens and green onions. 5—Lower the heat to the minimum and keep cooking for 1 to 2 minutes. Serve immediately.

The longer you let the flavors infuse, the better the soup is. If you choose to prepare it in advance and reheat later, reserve the chrysanthemum greens and green onions and add just before serving.

SHRIMP AND YAM SOUP (YAM PI)
— CANH KHOAI MỠ

Serves 4 to 6 ✦ Prep time 15 minutes ✦ Cook time 20 minutes

Peanut oil, for cooking
¼ lb (110 g) ground pork
1 lb (454 g) raw shrimp, peeled and
   coarsely chopped
½ cup (60 g) minced onions
6 cups (1.5 L) water
2½ Tbsp (37.5 mL) fish sauce

2 cups (300 g) grated yam (fresh or frozen)
Freshly ground black pepper
2 green onions, white and green parts,
   minced
½ cup (30 g) chopped fresh cilantro leaves
½ cup (30 g) chopped rice paddy herbs

1—Heat a splash of oil in a stockpot set over high heat. Fry the pork, shrimp, and the
½ cup (60 g) minced onions until lightly browned. 2—Add the water and fish sauce,
bring to a boil, and cook for 2 minutes, skimming as needed. 3—Add the grated yam,
generously season with black pepper, and keep cooking for 5 minutes. 4—Stir in the green
onions, cilantro, and rice paddy herbs, then remove from heat and serve immediately.

SWEET AND SOUR SOUP
— CANH CHUA CÁ

Serves 4 to 6 ✦ Prep time 40 minutes + resting ✦ Cook time 15 minutes

3 Tbsp (75 g) tamarind paste

¾ cup (180 mL) boiling water

6 cups (1.5 L) water

3 Tbsp (45 mL) fish sauce

1¼ lb (560 g) tilapia fillets (or another firm-fleshed fish)

¼ fresh pineapple, peeled and cored

2 ripe tomatoes, cut into quarters

8 to 10 fresh okra, sliced

1 stalk taro, peeled and sliced

Salt and freshly ground black pepper

1½ cups (150 g) bean sprouts

1 bunch rice paddy herbs, coarsely chopped

1 bunch fresh cilantro, coarsely chopped

Fried onions or garlic, to taste

Bird's eye chili, thinly sliced, for serving

Fish sauce dressing, for serving (p. 23)

1—Spoon the tamarind paste into a bowl and cover with the boiling water. Let stand for 15 minutes. 2—Pour the 6 cups (1.5 L) water into a stockpot, then add the fish sauce. 3—Pour the tamarind paste and water mixture through a sieve into the stockpot. With a spoon, press down on the tamarind flesh to extract as much pulp as possible. Discard the seeds and residual pulp. 4—Stir to combine and bring to a boil. 5—Add the fish fillets to the broth and cook for 5 minutes. Remove the fish and reserve. 6—Slice the pineapple lengthwise, then cut each piece into ½-inch (1.2 cm) thick slices. 7—Add the pineapple and tomatoes to the broth and bring back to a boil. 8—Add the okra and taro, lightly season with salt and pepper, and keep cooking for 2 minutes. 9—Add the fish back to the pot, then stir in the bean sprouts, rice paddy herbs and cilantro. Bring back to a simmer, then remove from heat. 10—Serve piping hot, sprinkled with fried onions or garlic, with bowls of bird's eye chili and fish sauce dressing to dip the fish in.

FISH AND TOMATO SOUP
— CANH MẮN

Serves 4 to 6 ✦ Prep time 15 minutes ✦ Cook time 10 minutes

1 whitefish fillet (about 1 lb/454 g)
2½ Tbsp (37.5 mL) fish sauce, divided
2 green onions, white and green parts, sliced
Freshly ground black pepper
6 cups (1.5 L) water

1 large ripe tomato, cut into quarters
1 stalk Chinese celery or lovage, sliced
Juice of ½ lime
1 handful fresh cilantro leaves

1—Drizzle the fish with half of the fish sauce. 2—Using the flat side of a chef's knife, crush the green onions and place on the fish fillet. 3—Generously season with black pepper and let rest for 10 minutes. 4—Add the water and the remaining fish sauce to a stockpot and bring to a boil. 5—Transfer the fish and its marinade to the pot, then add the tomatoes and celery. Bring back to a boil and cook for 3 minutes. 6—Remove from heat, then stir in the lime juice and cilantro. Serve immediately.

INSTANT BEEF SOUP
— CANH BÒ RÂM

Serves 4 to 6 ✦ Prep time 5 minutes ✦ Cook time 10 minutes

6 cups (1.5 L) water

2½ Tbsp (37.5 mL) fish sauce

½ lb (225 g) beef strip loin, thinly sliced

1 tomato, diced

2 green onions, white and green parts,
    sliced into ½-inch (1.2 cm) pieces

Juice of ½ lime

Freshly ground black pepper

Vietnamese coriander, to taste

1—Add the water and fish sauce to a stockpot and bring to a boil. 2—Place the beef, tomatoes, and green onions in a serving bowl. 3—Pour the piping-hot broth straight over the beef and vegetables. 4—Stir in the lime juice and generously season with black pepper. Garnish with Vietnamese coriander and serve immediately.

AUNT 5 — *LÝ KIM HẢI*

During their inevitably tense meetings, the mediator who handled Aunt 5's divorce was amazed to see her always calm and smiling when asked questions that were often difficult and demanding.

Aunt 5 explained to us that she smiled in order to have time to mentally conjugate French verbs without displaying her panic at the choice between *être* and *avoir* in the simple past tense, the total transformation required for irregular verbs, or the difference between the imperfect and the future perfect tense. Because, unlike French, Vietnamese always uses the infinitive. We orient ourselves with words indicating time, such as "tomorrow," "yesterday," "January." We insert these terms sporadically into the conversation or once at the very beginning. Otherwise there are no verb tenses as such. It may be due to that structure of the Vietnamese language that we are unconsciously always in a single time.

BOWLS AND STIR-FRIES

DRESSED VERMICELLI BOWLS
— BÚN

Serves 2 ✦ Prep time 15 minutes ✦ Cook time depends on chosen stir-fry recipe

2 large curly lettuce leaves

2 handfuls fresh herbs (e.g., Thai basil,
   cilantro, Vietnamese coriander,
   mint, shiso)

2 cups (350 g) cooked rice vermicelli

1 cucumber, julienned

1 cup (100 g) bean sprouts

½ cup (125 mL) Vietnamese pickled
   vegetables (p. 31)

2 servings stir-fried protein (beef, pork,
   chicken, or tofu; recipes pp. 57 to 70)

Dipping fish sauce (p. 23), to taste
   + more for serving

Green onion sauce (p. 24), to taste

Crushed peanuts, to taste

Fried shallots, to taste (see note)

1—Lay the lettuce leaves flat on a cutting board. Divide the fresh herbs between the lettuce leaves, then roll each leaf tightly. Slice the rolls thinly and set this chiffonade aside. 2—Divide the vermicelli between two large serving bowls, then set the following side by side: lettuce and herb chiffonade, cucumber, bean sprouts, pickled vegetables, and the stir-fry of your choice. 3—Drizzle each bowl with dipping fish sauce and garnish with green onion sauce, crushed peanuts, and fried shallots. Serve immediately, with small bowls of dipping fish sauce on the side.

For the fried shallot garnish, peel and slice a handful of shallots and fry in a splash of vegetable oil in a pan over medium heat until browned and crispy.

GARLIC BEEF STIR-FRY
— BÒ XÀO

Serves 2 ✦ Prep time 10 minutes ✦ Cook time 8 minutes

½ lb (225 g) beef sirloin or tenderloin,
   cut into strips
1 small clove garlic, minced
½ Tbsp (7.5 mL) fish sauce

Freshly ground black pepper
Peanut oil, for cooking
1 onion, cut into eighths
2 dressed vermicelli bowls (p. 56)

1—In a stainless-steel bowl, combine the beef, garlic, and fish sauce. Season with black pepper and let stand for 5 minutes. 2—Heat a splash of oil in a wok set over high heat, then add the onions and sauté until lightly browned. 3—Add the beef and fry for 2 minutes, stirring constantly. 4—Divide between the vermicelli bowls and serve immediately.

LEMONGRASS PORK STIR-FRY
— HEO XÀO SẢ

Serves 2 ✦ Prep time 5 minutes + marinating ✦ Cook time 3 minutes

½ lb (225 g) pork belly, sliced into strips

1 small clove garlic, minced

½ Tbsp (7.5 mL) fish sauce

2 tsp (2 g) minced fresh lemongrass

Freshly ground black pepper

Vegetable oil, for cooking

½ onion, sliced

2 dressed vermicelli bowls (p. 56)

1—In a stainless-steel bowl, combine the pork belly, garlic, fish sauce, and lemongrass. Season with black pepper and let stand for 5 minutes. 2—Place a wok over high heat, add a splash of oil, and sauté the pork mixture and onions for 3 minutes, stirring constantly, until golden. 3—Divide between the vermicelli bowls and serve immediately.

You can substitute chicken strips for the pork belly.

LEMONGRASS TOFU CUBES
— ĐẬU HỦ CHIÊN SẢ

Serves 2 ✦ Prep time 10 minutes ✦ Cook time 15 minutes

⅔ cup (40 g) minced fresh lemongrass

1 tsp (6 g) salt

1 bird's eye chili, minced

1 block (1 lb/454 g) medium-firm tofu,
   cut into 1-inch (2.5 cm) cubes

¼ cup (60 mL) peanut oil

1 clove garlic, minced

2 dressed vermicelli bowls (p. 56)

1—To a medium-size stainless-steel bowl, add the lemongrass, salt, and bird's eye chili. Stir to combine, then add the tofu cubes and toss to coat. 2—Heat the oil in a heavy-bottomed skillet set over medium heat. Add the tofu cubes and sauté until golden on all sides. 3—Add the garlic and cook for 5 more minutes, tossing the tofu cubes a few times every so often. 4—Divide the tofu cubes between the two vermicelli bowls and serve immediately.

CHAYOTE, PORK, AND SHRIMP STIR-FRY
— SU SU XÀO

Serves 4 ✦ Prep time 20 minutes ✦ Cook time 10 minutes

½ lb (225 g) raw shrimp, peeled
½ lb (225 g) pork belly, thinly sliced
1 clove garlic, minced
3 Tbsp (45 mL) fish sauce, divided
Freshly ground black pepper
Vegetable oil, for cooking
1 to 2 chayote, peeled, pitted, and cut into
 matchsticks

½ onion, sliced
3 green onions, white and green parts,
 sliced into 1-inch (2.5 cm) pieces
Fresh cilantro, to taste
Dipping fish sauce (p. 23), to taste
 + more for serving

1—Slice each shrimp in half lengthwise. 2—In a stainless-steel bowl, place the shrimp, pork belly, and garlic. Add 1 tablespoon (15 mL) of the fish sauce, then generously season with black pepper. Toss to combine and allow to marinate while you prepare the remaining stir-fry ingredients. 3—Heat a splash of oil in a large skillet set over medium-high heat. Add the shrimp and pork mixture and sauté for 5 minutes. Remove from skillet and set aside. 4—Add more oil to the skillet if needed, then add the chayote and sliced onions (not the green onions) and cook until softened. 5—Return the shrimp and pork mixture to the skillet, add the remaining fish sauce and the green onions, and toss to combine. 6—Garnish with cilantro and serve immediately, with dipping fish sauce on the side.

If you like, you can substitute 2 cups (250 g) of green beans for the chayote.

MARINATED PORK BELLY AND BAMBOO SHOOTS
— MĂNG XÀO

Serves 4 ✦ Prep time 15 minutes + marinating ✦ Cook time 15 minutes

1 lb (454 g) pork belly, cut into ¼-inch
  (6 mm) thick slices
3 Tbsp (45 mL) fish sauce
1 clove garlic, minced
1 bird's eye chili, sliced
1 onion, cut into eighths
Freshly ground black pepper

2 cans (8 oz/227 mL each) sliced bamboo
  shoots
Vegetable oil, for cooking
3 green onions, white and green parts,
  slivered, divided
Fresh cilantro
Dipping fish sauce (p. 23), for serving

1—Place the pork belly in a stainless-steel bowl, then add the fish sauce, garlic, chili, and onions. Season with black pepper, stir to combine, and refrigerate for 15 minutes. 2—Rinse the bamboo shoots several times, then drain well and set aside. 3—Heat a splash of oil in a large skillet set over high heat. Add the pork and marinade and sauté until the pork is golden brown. 4—Add the bamboo shoots and keep cooking for 2 minutes. 5—Add half of the green onions and stir to incorporate. 6—Garnish with cilantro and the remaining green onions and serve immediately, with small bowls of dipping fish sauce on the side.

BEEF CUBE STIR-FRY
— BÒ LÚC LẮC

Serves 1 ✦ Prep time 5 minutes ✦ Cook time 2 minutes

¼ lb (110 g) beef sirloin, cut into bite-size
    cubes
1 tsp (5 mL) Maggi sauce
Freshly ground black pepper
Peanut oil, for cooking
1 clove garlic, minced

Salt
1 handful watercress
1 small tomato, sliced
Pickled shallots (p. 31), to taste
1 bowl cooked jasmine rice (p. 29)

1—In a stainless-steel bowl, combine the beef cubes and Maggi sauce. Generously season with black pepper. Set aside. 2—Place a wok over high heat, then add a splash of oil. Add the garlic and sauté for 30 seconds. 3—Add the reserved beef, season with salt, and keep cooking for 1 more minute, stirring constantly. 4—Spoon the beef over a bed of watercress and garnish with tomato slices and pickled shallots. Serve with jasmine rice.

You should stir-fry only one serving at a time to make sure it stays piping hot throughout the process.

CARAMEL PORK
— THỊT RAM

Serves 4 ✦ Prep time 20 minutes ✦ Cook time 15 minutes

5 Tbsp (60 g) sugar

3 Tbsp (45 mL) water, divided

2 cloves garlic, minced

1 onion, minced

¼ lb (110 g) pork belly (rind on), cut into
 ¼-inch (6 mm) thick slices

1 lb (454 g) pork loin, cut into strips

1 bird's eye chili, minced

Freshly ground black pepper

3 Tbsp (45 mL) fish sauce

2 green onions, white and green parts,
 chopped

Fresh cilantro leaves

1—Combine the sugar and 1 tablespoon (15 mL) of the water in a stockpot. Set over medium heat and boil until the sugar turns into a deep amber caramel. 2—Increase heat to medium-high, then add the garlic, onions, and pork belly. Cook, stirring constantly, for 5 minutes. 3—Add the pork loin strips and bird's eye chili, then generously season with black pepper. Stir well to coat all the ingredients with caramel. 4—Add the remaining water and the fish sauce, and keep cooking, stirring frequently, until the sauce has a slightly syrupy texture. 5—Serve immediately, garnished with the green onions and cilantro.

The best sidekicks to this dish are a few slices of cucumber or pieces of blanched cabbage.

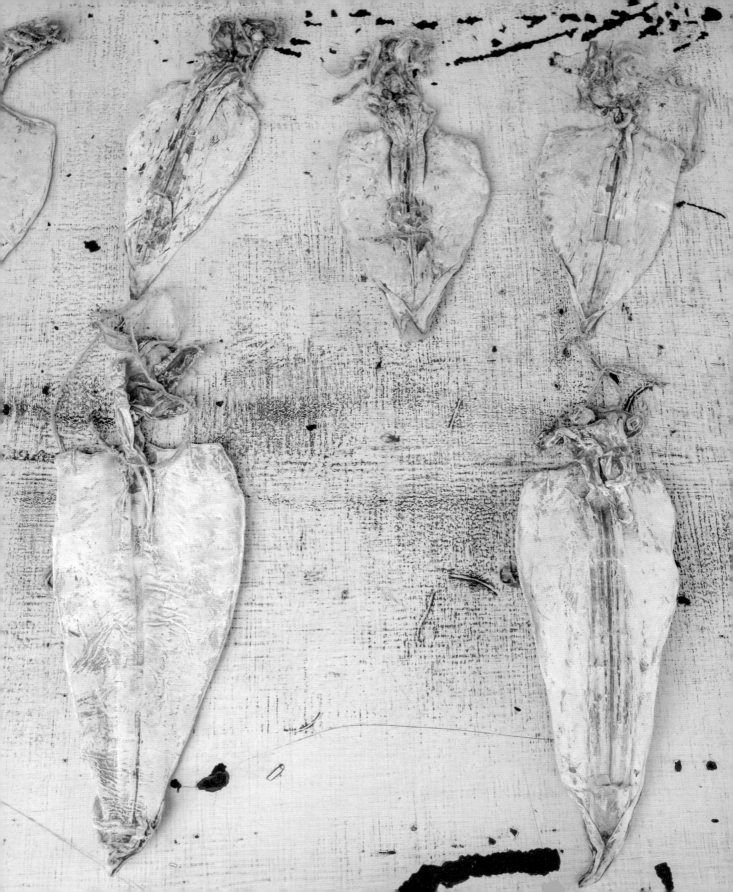

All through my early childhood, we went to the sea almost every month for "a change of wind," as my father said. The salt water miraculously healed the cracked skin on my grandmother's heels, and cleared up my own frequently congested nose. The salt air helped my brothers grow, and amplified our laughter around the dried cuttlefish sold on the beach by itinerant merchants. Two cuttlefish, perfectly flat and grilled over a few red coals, fed the whole family for the whole afternoon, since they were eaten strand by strand. The taste of these elastic filaments lasted longer than a stick of Juicy Fruit in my mouth.

—from the novel *Vi* by Kim Thúy

CALAMARI, CUCUMBER, AND PINEAPPLE STIR-FRY
— MỰC XÀO

Serves 4 to 6 ✦ Prep time 20 minutes ✦ Cook time 15 minutes

1 lb (454 g) U10 calamari tubes

¼ fresh pineapple, peeled and cored

Vegetable oil, for cooking

1 onion, sliced

2 cloves garlic, minced

2 tomatoes, cut into eight wedges

1 cucumber, peeled, seeded, and sliced into
   half-moons

3 Tbsp (45 mL) fish sauce

2 Tbsp (30 mL) rice vinegar

2 stalks Chinese celery, coarsely chopped

Freshly ground black pepper

Fresh cilantro, to taste

Dipping fish sauce (p. 23), for serving

1—Pat the calamari tubes dry. Cut open one side of each calamari and pat the insides dry.
2—Using a very sharp knife, score the inside surface of each calamari in a diamond pattern,
being careful not to cut all the way through. Cut each scored calamari into 2-inch (5 cm)
squares. Set aside. 3—Slice the pineapple in half lengthwise, then cut each piece into
½-inch (1.2 cm) thick pieces. 4—Heat a splash of oil in a large nonstick skillet set over high
heat. Add the calamari, smooth side down, and cook for 2 minutes, or until each piece curls
up onto itself. Remove and set aside. 5—Add more oil to the skillet, if necessary, then sauté
the onions and garlic for 1 minute. 6—Add the tomatoes, pineapple, and cucumber, and
cook for 2 minutes. 7—Pour in the fish sauce and rice vinegar, then add the Chinese celery.
Season generously with black pepper and keep cooking, stirring constantly, until the
vegetables are crisp-tender. Stir in the reserved calamari. 8—Garnish with cilantro and
serve immediately, with small bowls of dipping fish sauce on the side.

You can replace the Chinese celery with lovage or regular celery leaves.
You can also substitute frozen calamari rings for the U10 calamari.

TAMARIND CRAB
— CUA RANG ME

Serves 2 ✦ Prep time 20 minutes, including resting ✦ Cook time 10 minutes

4 Tbsp (100 g) tamarind paste
1 cup (250 mL) boiling water
2 Tbsp (30 mL) fish sauce
2 Tbsp (25 g) sugar
Peanut oil, for cooking

1 clove garlic, minced
1½ lb (675 g) shell-on snow crab, chopped
  into pieces
2 green onions, white and green parts,
  sliced into rounds

1—Spoon the tamarind paste into a heatproof bowl and cover with boiling water. Stir and let stand for 10 minutes. 2—Once time has elapsed, pour the tamarind paste and water mixture through a strainer into a small saucepan. Using the back of a spoon, press down on the tamarind flesh to extract as much as possible. Discard the seeds and residual pulp. 3—Bring the tamarind liquid to a boil and cook until reduced by half. Mix in the fish sauce and sugar. Set aside. 4—Heat a splash of oil in a wok set over high heat. Add the garlic and sauté for 30 seconds. 5—Add the crab and cook for 1 more minute, stirring constantly. 6—Add the tamarind syrup and cook for 1 minute, turning the crab over a few times to coat it with the sauce. 7—Stir in the green onions. Serve hot.

AUNT 6 — *LÝ KIM HIẾU*

*As a girl, she would often use the tip of a toothpick to draw
a line just above the contour of her eye to make an eyelid.*

She was the most daring girl in the family. All of five feet tall, she dressed in bell-bottoms or miniskirts. Her favorite T-shirt was red with an enormous royal blue heart that covered her chest. She took our photos as if we were fashion models or Hollywood stars. She studied to become a French teacher and I was her first pupil: "*La souris est sur la table; la souris est sous la table.*" She could not imagine that one day she would be at sea on a makeshift boat with a five-month-old baby, and that she would go on to live in the United States, and work in English at a large company, with a big salary—when she had once dreamed of becoming a painter, an artist.

VEGETABLES

VIETNAMESE EGGPLANT
— CÀ TÍM NƯỚNG

Serves 4 to 6 ♣ Prep time 15 minutes ♣ Cook time 30 minutes

1 lb (454 g) small Asian eggplants

¼ cup (60 mL) fish sauce dressing (p. 23)

½ batch green onion sauce (p. 24)

2 Tbsp (30 mL) fried garlic

Bird's eye chili, thinly sliced, to taste

1—Preheat the oven to 350°F (180°C). 2—With a fork, prick the eggplant skin several times. Set the eggplants on a baking sheet, then bake for 30 minutes or until the flesh is thoroughly cooked. Let the eggplants cool. 3—Once the eggplants are cool enough to handle, remove the stalk, then cut into bite-size cubes. Transfer to a serving dish. 4—Drizzle with fish sauce dressing, toss to coat, then garnish with green onion sauce, fried garlic, and some bird's eye chili.

You can also use Italian eggplants to make this recipe. If you use large eggplants, cook them a little longer and remove the skin before cutting the flesh into cubes.

EGGPLANT, PORK, AND SHRIMP
— CÀ TÍM TÔM THỊT

Serves 4 to 6 ✦ Prep time 10 minutes ✦ Cook time 35 minutes

1 lb (454 g) small Asian eggplants
¾ lb (340 g) ground pork
¼ lb (110 g) raw shrimp, peeled and finely
   chopped
1 Tbsp (15 mL) fish sauce

Freshly ground black pepper
Vegetable oil, for cooking
Green onion sauce (p. 24), to taste
Dipping fish sauce (p. 23), for serving

1—Preheat the oven to 350°F (180°C). 2—With a fork, prick the eggplant skin several times. Set the eggplants on a baking sheet, then bake for 30 minutes or until the flesh is thoroughly cooked. Let the eggplants cool. 3—Once the eggplants are cool enough to handle, remove the stalk, then cut into bite-size cubes. 4—Put the pork and shrimp in a bowl, drizzle with fish sauce, season with black pepper, and toss to combine. 5—Heat a splash of oil in a large skillet set over medium-high heat. Add the shrimp and pork mixture and sauté for 5 minutes. 6—Stir in the eggplant cubes, then drizzle with green onion sauce. 7—Serve with small bowls of dipping fish sauce on the side.

STIR-FRIED WATER SPINACH WITH GARLIC
— RAU MUỐNG XÀO TỎI

Serves 4 ✦ Prep time 10 minutes ✦ Cook time 5 minutes

1 lb (454 g) fresh water spinach

2 Tbsp (30 mL) vegetable oil, for cooking

3 cloves garlic, minced

2 Tbsp (30 mL) fish sauce

1—Chop the water spinach into three or four pieces. 2—Heat the oil in a wok set over medium-high heat. Add the garlic and fry for 30 seconds. 3—Add the water spinach and sauté for 2 minutes. 4—Drizzle with fish sauce, toss to combine, and serve immediately.

CHICKEN SLAW
— GỎI GÀ BẮP CẢI TRẮNG

Serves 4 ✦ Prep time 20 minutes, including resting

4 cups (400 g) shredded cabbage
½ Tbsp (9 g) salt
¼ cup (60 mL) pickled shallots (p. 31)
1½ cups (250 g) shredded roasted, boiled,
   or grilled chicken meat

¼ cup (60 mL) fish sauce dressing (p. 23)
½ cup (30 g) coarsely chopped Vietnamese
   coriander
¼ cup (30 g) crushed peanuts

1—Place the cabbage in a bowl, sprinkle with salt, and toss to combine. Let stand for 15 minutes. 2—Transfer the cabbage to a colander and rinse under cold running water. Drain thoroughly. 3—Place the cabbage, pickled shallots, and chicken in a salad bowl and drizzle with the fish sauce dressing. Toss to combine. 4—Garnish with the Vietnamese coriander and peanuts. Serve immediately.

BEAN SPROUT SALAD
— GỎI GIÁ

Serves 4 to 6 ◆ Prep time 5 minutes

¼ cup (60 mL) rice vinegar

1 tsp (4 g) sugar

2 cups (200 g) bean sprouts

3 stalks garlic chives, coarsely chopped

Salt

1—Toss all the ingredients together in a salad bowl, mixing well.

This salad is the perfect accompaniment to caramel pork stew (p. 126).

VEGETABLE RIBBON, PORK, AND SHRIMP SALAD
— *GỎI RAU CỦ*

Serves 4 ✦ Prep time 15 minutes + resting ✦ Cook time 7 minutes

1 small daikon, shaved into ribbons using a mandoline (or vegetable peeler)

2 carrots, shaved into ribbons using a mandoline (or vegetable peeler)

1 stalk celery, shaved into ribbons using a mandoline (or vegetable peeler)

¼ lb (110 g) raw shrimp

¼ lb (110 g) pork belly

1 to 2 cucumbers

⅓ cup (85 mL) fish sauce dressing (p. 23), divided

Handful Thai basil, coarsely chopped

Handful Vietnamese coriander, coarsely chopped

Bird's eye chili, thinly sliced, to taste

¼ cup (30 g) crushed peanuts

2 Tbsp (30 mL) fried shallots (p. 56)

1—Add the daikon, carrot, and celery ribbons to a bowl of ice water and refrigerate for 15 minutes. 2—Bring 4 cups (1 L) of salted water to a boil. Add the shrimp and cook for 2 minutes. 3—Using a slotted spoon, transfer the shrimp to a bowl of ice water. (Keep the pot of water boiling.) 4—Add the pork belly to the pot of boiling water and cook for 5 minutes, skimming regularly. 5—Meanwhile, peel the shrimp, then slice in half lengthwise. Transfer to a salad bowl and refrigerate. 6—Using a slotted spoon, transfer the pork belly to a bowl and refrigerate. 7—Strain the cooking water into a heatproof, airtight container and store, refrigerated, for another use. 8—Once the pork belly is cold, slice into strips and add to the salad bowl. 9—Drain the vegetable ribbons, cut the cucumbers into matchsticks, and add all the vegetables to the salad bowl. 10—Drizzle with half of the fish sauce dressing. Add the Thai basil, Vietnamese coriander, and bird's eye chili. Toss to combine. 11—Refrigerate for 10 minutes. 12—When ready to serve, adjust seasoning by adding more dressing to taste. Garnish with crushed peanuts and fried shallots and serve immediately.

If you like, you can add thinly sliced green mango to this salad.

LOTUS ROOT SALAD
— GỎI SEN

Serves 4 ✦ Prep time 30 minutes ✦ Cook time 7 minutes

¼ lb (110 g) raw shrimp
¼ lb (110 g) pork belly
1 jar (16 oz/454 g) lotus roots
¼ cup (60 mL) fish sauce dressing (p. 23)

1 handful Vietnamese coriander, coarsely
  chopped
Bird's eye chili, thinly sliced, to taste
¼ cup (30 g) crushed peanuts
2 Tbsp (30 mL) fried shallots (p. 56)

1—In a small saucepan, bring salted water to a boil. Add the shrimp and cook for 2 minutes. Using a slotted spoon, transfer the shrimp to a bowl of ice water. (Keep the saucepan of water boiling.) 2—Add the pork belly to the pot of boiling water and cook for 5 minutes, skimming regularly. Using a slotted spoon, transfer the pork belly to a dish and refrigerate. 3—Meanwhile, peel the shrimp, then slice in half lengthwise. Transfer to a salad bowl. Set aside. 4—Strain the cooking water into a heatproof, airtight container and store, refrigerated, for another use. 5—Cut the lotus roots into thin slices and add to the salad bowl with the reserved shrimp. 6—Once the pork belly is cold, slice into thin strips and add to the salad bowl. 7—Add the fish sauce dressing, Vietnamese coriander, and bird's eye chili, then toss to combine. 8—Garnish with the peanuts and fried shallots. Serve immediately.

WARM WATER SPINACH AND BEEF SALAD
— GỎI RAU MUỐNG

Serves 4 to 6 ✦ Prep time 30 minutes, including resting ✦ Cook time 5 minutes

1 bunch water spinach

Peanut oil, for cooking

1 onion, thickly sliced

1 clove garlic, minced

½ lb (225 g) beef sirloin, thinly sliced

2 Tbsp (30 mL) fish sauce

¼ cup (60 mL) pickled shallots (p. 31)

¼ cup (30 g) crushed peanuts

Dipping fish sauce (p. 23), for serving

1—With a sharp knife, slice the water spinach into long shreds, transferring them to a large bowl of cold water as you go. 2—Once the shreds are all curled up, transfer to a colander to drain for a few minutes, tossing from time to time. 3—Heat a splash of oil in a nonstick skillet set over high heat, add the onions and garlic, and sauté for 1 minute. 4—Add the beef and sauté for 1 minute. 5—Drizzle with the fish sauce and toss to combine. 6—Transfer the curly water spinach to a salad bowl. Add the beef and its cooking liquid, the pickled shallots, and the crushed peanuts, and toss to combine. 7—Serve warm, with small bowls of dipping fish sauce on the side.

You can replace the water spinach with watercress or curly chicory.

AUNT 7 — *LÝ KIM HẠNH*

*What she adores is not the fried foods
themselves but the action of frying them.*

She likes to watch the oil bubbling, to stand next to the stove turning the sticks of sweet potato fries, rolls of sesame dough, a slice of breaded eggplant . . . It's the aroma that hypnotizes her—or maybe it's the danger. Frying represents a risk that she knows all too well: she burned herself when she accidentally spilled a kettle of boiling oil onto her hand. Many things in life confound her: she can't add numbers in her head, or measure out 100 grams of flour, or live alone. But her fried bananas are superlative, and she masters the art of conversation better than all of her sisters.

GRILLED AND FRIED

FRIED CHICKEN WINGS
— CÁNH GÀ CHIÊN

Serves 4 ✦ Prep time 10 minutes + marinating ✦ Cook time 15 minutes

1 lb (454 g) chicken wings, split in half
1 clove garlic, minced
¼ cup (60 mL) fish sauce
Freshly ground black pepper

Peanut oil, for frying
1 cup (150 g) rice flour or (128 g) cornstarch
Banana leaves, for serving (optional)

1—Combine the chicken wings, garlic, and fish sauce in a stainless-steel bowl. Generously season with black pepper and let rest for 5 minutes. 2—Cover the bottom of a large stainless-steel skillet with ⅓ inch (1 cm) oil. Set over medium-high heat. 3—Place the rice flour in another stainless-steel bowl. 4—Remove the chicken wings from the marinade, quickly shaking excess liquid off them, then dredge in the flour. 5—Set the chicken wings side by side in the hot oil and cook for 10 to 15 minutes, until the wings are golden brown and cooked through. 6—Transfer the chicken wings to a banana leaf or a serving plate and serve immediately.

FROG LEGS
— ĐÙI ẾCH BƠ TỎI

Serves 4 ♣ Prep time 10 minutes ♣ Cook time 10 minutes

Salt and freshly ground black pepper
1 cup (150 g) rice flour
1 lb (454 g) frog legs

Vegetable oil, for cooking
½ cup (113 g) salted butter, divided
2 cloves garlic, chopped

1—In a stainless-steel bowl, combine the salt, black pepper, and rice flour. 2—Dredge the frog legs in the flour mixture. 3—Add a generous drizzle of oil to a large stainless-steel skillet set over medium-high heat. Sauté the frog legs until they're nicely golden on both sides. 4—In another skillet, melt 2 tablespoons (28 g) of the butter over high heat. Add the garlic and fry until it begins to color. 5—Add the remaining butter, lower the heat, and cook until completely melted. 6—Transfer the frog legs to a serving plate. Drizzle with the garlic butter and serve immediately.

SALMON STEAKS, TWO WAYS
— CÁ CHIÊN

Serves 4 ✦ Prep time 15 minutes ✦ Cook time 10 minutes

Peanut oil, for frying
4 salmon steaks (about 6 oz/170 g each)
Salt and freshly ground black pepper

Tomato topping (p. 102) or mango and ginger
   topping (p. 102)
1 handful fresh cilantro leaves
2 cups (500 mL) cooked jasmine rice (p. 29)

1—Cover the bottom of a large stainless-steel skillet with ⅓ inch (1 cm) oil. Set over medium-high heat. Season the salmon steaks with salt and pepper, then fry for 3 minutes on each side. 2—Transfer the salmon to a plate covered with two layers of paper towel. 3—To serve, transfer the salmon steaks to a large serving plate and garnish with your choice of topping and some cilantro leaves. Serve immediately with jasmine rice.

The Vietnamese often cook whole fish because they love the crunch of fried fins and tails.

TOMATO TOPPING
— SỐT CÀ

Prep time 10 minutes ♦ Cook time 10 minutes

Peanut oil, for cooking

1 green bell pepper, diced

2 large ripe tomatoes, diced

1 carrot, grated

1 Tbsp (15 mL) fish sauce

Freshly ground black pepper

Dipping fish sauce (p. 23), for serving

Bird's eye chili, minced, for serving

1—Add a splash of oil to a small skillet and set over medium-high heat. Add the bell pepper and cook for 5 minutes, without letting it brown. 2—Add the tomatoes and keep cooking for 1 minute. Stir in the grated carrot and fish sauce. Season with black pepper and stir well to combine. Cook for 1 more minute, then remove from heat. 3—Serve the topping warm over the salmon steaks (p. 101), with dipping fish sauce and bird's eye chili on the side.

MANGO AND GINGER TOPPING
— XOÀI CHUA

Prep time 10 minutes

3 Tbsp (45 mL) dipping fish sauce

2 Tbsp (12 g) pureed or grated ginger

1 clove garlic, minced

1 mango (green, if available), peeled, pitted, and julienned

Cilantro

Bird's eye chili, minced, to taste

1—In a small bowl, combine the dipping fish sauce, ginger, and garlic. 2—Place the salmon steaks (p. 101) on a serving dish and top with the julienned mango. 3—Spoon the ginger fish sauce mixture over the mango and garnish with cilantro and chili. Serve immediately.

FRIED LEMONGRASS FISH
— CÁ CHIÊN SẢ

Serves 4 ✦ Prep time 25 minutes, including resting ✦ Cook time 10 minutes

1 lb (454 g) small white-fleshed fish
  (smelts, butterfish, anchovies)
⅔ cup (40 g) minced fresh lemongrass
1 tsp (6 g) salt
1 bird's eye chili, minced

Peanut oil, for cooking
1 clove garlic, minced
2 cups (500 mL) cooked jasmine rice (p. 29)
Dipping fish sauce, for serving (p. 23)

1—Clean, wash, and thoroughly dry the fish. 2—Combine the lemongrass, salt, and bird's eye chili in a shallow dish, then roll the fish into the mixture. Let stand for 5 minutes, then roll the fish into the lemongrass mixture again. 3—Cover the bottom of a large stainless-steel skillet with ⅓ inch (1 cm) oil. Set over medium-high heat. Add the fish and fry until golden brown on both sides. 4—Add the garlic and fry for 2 more minutes, turning the fish a few more times. 5—Serve immediately with jasmine rice and small bowls of dipping fish sauce.

There were many words whose meaning Maman didn't know. Luckily, we had ready access to a living dictionary. He was older than Maman. The neighbors thought he was crazy because every day he stood under the rose apple tree, where he recited words in French and their definitions. His dictionary, which he had held close to him throughout his childhood, had been confiscated, but he went on turning the pages in his head. I just had to say a word to him through the fence that separated us and he would give me the definition. And one time, he had given me the rosiest of the rose apples from the bunch that hung just above his head when I gave him the verb *to sniff*.

"Sniff: to breathe in through the nose in order to smell. To sniff the air. The wind. The fog. To sniff the fruit! Sniff! Rose apple, in Guyana known also as love apple. Sniff!"

After that lesson, I never ate a love apple without first sniffing the glossy, fuchsia-pink skin, its innocent coolness nearly hypnotic.

—from the novel *Mãn* by Kim Thúy

105

BEEF IN BETEL LEAVES
— *BÒ LÁ LỐT*

Makes about 30 rolls ♣ Prep time 40 minutes + marinating ♣ Cook time 10 to 30 minutes

1 lb (454 g) ground beef	Salt
½ lb (225 g) ground pork	¼ cup (60 mL) soy sauce
½ cup (60 g) coarsely chopped peanuts	3 Tbsp (45 mL) rum
1 clove garlic, minced	30 large betel leaves
3 Tbsp (9 g) minced fresh lemongrass	Dipping fish sauce (p. 23), for serving

1—In a large stainless-steel bowl, combine the beef, pork, peanuts, garlic, and lemongrass. Lightly season with salt and mix well. 2—Drizzle the soy sauce and rum over the meat mixture and mix to combine. Cover with plastic wrap and refrigerate for 30 minutes. 3—Set a betel leaf flat on a work surface. Add a spoonful of the meat mixture in the center of the leaf, then roll it tightly and stick the stalk into the leaf blade to seal the roll. Repeat the steps to make all the rolls. 4—Cook the rolls on a grill pan or on the barbecue at medium-high for 10 to 15 minutes, turning them regularly. Alternatively, you can preheat the oven to 350°F (180°C), set the rolls on an aluminum foil–lined baking sheet, and bake for 30 minutes. 5—Serve with small bowls of dipping fish sauce.

If you can't find betel leaves, you can use kale leaves instead.

PORK AND BEEF SKEWERS
— XIÊNG BÒ & HEO NƯỚNG

Serves 4 ✦ Prep time 20 minutes + 1 hour marinating ✦ Cook time 6 minutes

1 lb (454 g) pork belly, rind on

1 lb (454 g) flank steak or brisket, rind on

8 Chinese (flat) bamboo skewers, soaked
   in water

½ cup (125 mL) fish sauce

½ cup (125 mL) maple syrup

½ cup (125 mL) water

2 cloves garlic, minced

1 small onion, minced

½ cup (30 g) minced fresh lemongrass
   or ¼ cup (24 g) minced fresh ginger

2 recipes dressed vermicelli bowls
   (4 bowls total) (p. 56)

Dipping fish sauce, to taste (p. 23)

1—Slice the pork and beef into thin slices, then thread the meat onto the skewers.
2—Transfer the skewers to a large rectangular container. 3—In a bowl, combine the
fish sauce, maple syrup, water, garlic, onions, and lemongrass. 4—Pour the marinade
over the skewers. Cover with plastic wrap and refrigerate for 1 hour, turning the skewers
after 30 minutes. 5—Remove the skewers from the marinade and cook on a grill pan,
or on the barbecue over direct heat, for 3 minutes on each side, until the skewers
are golden and caramelized. 6—Transfer two skewers to each dressed vermicelli bowl.
7—Remove the meat from the skewers, drizzle with the dipping fish sauce, and toss
to combine.

Some diners may prefer to leave the meat on the skewer to nibble on.

VIETNAMESE GROUND PORK MEATBALLS IN RICE PAPER ROLLS
— NEM NƯỚNG

Makes 16 skewers ✦ Prep time 30 minutes ✦ Cook time 10 minutes

2 lb (900 g) ground pork

2 Tbsp (18 g) toasted rice flour
  (p. 27 or store-bought)

1 Tbsp (12 g) sugar

1 Tbsp (15 mL) rum

½ Tbsp (7 g) baking powder

1 Tbsp (15 mL) fish sauce

1 clove garlic, minced

Salt

16 Chinese (flat) bamboo skewers,
  soaked in water

Green onion sauce (p. 24), to taste

¼ cup (30 g) crushed peanuts

1 batch flavored hoisin sauce (p. 25)

1 vermicelli, vegetable, and fresh
  herb platter (p. 32)

1 package rice paper wrappers

1—In a large stainless-steel bowl, combine the ground pork, toasted rice flour, sugar, rum, baking powder, fish sauce, and garlic. Season with salt and mix thoroughly with your hands. 2—Divide the mixture into ¼-cup (60 mL) balls, then shape into rolls about 1 inch (2.5 cm) in diameter. 3—Thread each roll onto a skewer, pressing firmly around the meat to secure it. 4—Heat a grill pan over high heat, or the barbecue to high, and cook the skewers for 10 minutes, rotating them regularly. 5—Transfer the skewers to a serving plate, drizzle with green onion sauce, and sprinkle with crushed peanuts. 6—Provide each guest with a dipping bowl of flavored hoisin sauce. Serve the skewer plate and the vermicelli, vegetable, and fresh herb platter in the center of the table, along with a pile of rice paper wrappers and a bowl of warm water. 7—Each guest should dip a rice paper wrapper in the warm water to soften it, then assemble his or her roll with the provided ingredients and dip in the flavored hoisin sauce.

OVEN-BAKED FISH IN RICE PAPER ROLLS
— CÁ NƯỚNG

Serves 6 to 8 ✦ Prep time 30 minutes ✦ Cook time 30 minutes

1 whole (about 3 lb/1.5 kg) striped bass

1 cup (250 mL) vegetable oil + more for brushing and toasting

Salt and freshly ground black pepper

1 cup (250 mL) tiny cubes of stale bread

½ cup (100 g) sugar

1 Tbsp (18 g) salt

12 to 15 green onions, white and green parts, sliced into rounds

1 cup (250 mL) dipping fish sauce (p. 23)

2 Tbsp (12 g) pureed or grated ginger

½ cup (60 g) crushed peanuts

1 vermicelli, vegetable, and fresh herb platter (p. 32)

1 package rice paper wrappers

1—Preheat the oven to 375°F (190°C). 2—Brush the inside and outside of the fish with oil, then season with salt and pepper. Place the fish on a parchment paper–lined baking sheet. Bake for 30 minutes. 3—Meanwhile, add a splash of oil to a skillet set over medium-high heat, then toast the bread cubes until golden. Transfer to a paper towel–lined plate and set aside. 4—Add the 1 cup (250 mL) of oil to a large stainless-steel skillet and place over medium-high heat. 5—Add the sugar and salt. Wait for a minute, then add the green onions. Stir to combine, bring just to a simmer, then remove from heat. 6—Combine the dipping fish sauce with the pureed ginger and divide the sauce between dipping bowls. 7—When the fish is done, transfer to a large serving plate. Drizzle with the prepared green onion sauce (step 5), then garnish with toasted bread cubes and crushed peanuts. 8—Provide each guest with a dipping bowl of ginger fish sauce. Serve the fish and the vermicelli, vegetable, and fresh herb platter in the center of the table, along with a pile of rice paper wrappers and a bowl of warm water. 9—Each guest should dip a rice paper wrapper in the warm water to soften it, then assemble his or her roll with the provided ingredients and dip in the ginger fish sauce.

This recipe can be prepared with fish fillets instead of a whole fish. Make sure to adjust the baking time accordingly.

AUNT 8 — *LÝ KIM NHÂN*

*I shared a room with her and slept in the same bed
for two years after we arrived in Canada.*

One night she asked me the meaning of "goddess." She told me that a Québécois traveling in the bus that she took at the same time every morning had finally found the courage to speak to her. They made a date to share a picnic in the park across from our apartment. It was summer and she had on ancient-Greek-style sandals with cords that wound around her feet and ankles. While they were sitting on the grass to eat, he had stroked her bare toes and said "goddess." Ever since, I dream about that word spoken by a suitor of the eternal beauty who is my Aunt 8.

SLOW COOKING

LEMONGRASS BEEF STEW
— BÒ KHO

Serves 6 ✦ Prep time 20 minutes ✦ Cook time 1 hour 45 minutes

1 (about 3 lb/1.5 kg) bone-in beef pot roast

Vegetable oil, for cooking

4 stalks fresh lemongrass

1 onion, cut into eighths

2 carrots, diced

1 Tbsp (6 g) Madras curry powder

1 Tbsp (6 g) five spice powder

2 ripe tomatoes, cut into eighths

4 cups (1 L) water

Salt and freshly ground black pepper

Flat rice noodles, cooked, for serving

1 batch Vietnamese pickled vegetables (p. 31)

Thai basil, for serving

1—Debone the roast and set the bone(s) aside. 2—Cut the meat into large cubes. 3—Add a splash of oil to a stockpot set over high heat, then add the bone(s) and fry until browned. Remove the bones and set aside. 4—Add more oil if needed, then add the beef and brown on all sides. Remove the beef and set aside. 5—Slice the lemongrass stalks in half lengthwise, then use the flat side of a chef's knife to bruise them. 6—Add more oil to the stockpot, then sauté the lemongrass stalks, onions, and carrots until lightly browned. 7—Transfer the beef and bones back to the stockpot. Sprinkle with the curry and five spice powders. Stir to combine. 8—Add the tomatoes and water. Season with salt and pepper, then bring to a simmer. Half-cover the pot and cook for 1 hour and 30 minutes, or until the meat is fork-tender. 9—Remove the lemongrass stalks. Serve the stew with flat rice noodles, pickled daikon, and a few sprigs of Thai basil.

For a delicious way to mop up the sauce, serve this stew with a baguette—it's an East-meets-West culinary match made in heaven!

BEEF AND ONION MEATLOAF
— THỊT BÒ CHƯNG

Serves 8 ✦ Prep time 15 minutes ✦ Cook time 1 hour

2 onions

2 lb (900 g) ground beef

3 cloves garlic, minced

¼ cup (60 mL) soy sauce + more
   for serving

Freshly ground black pepper

2 to 3 cucumbers, cut into sticks

Cooked jasmine rice (p. 29)

Bird's eye chili, thinly sliced, for serving

1—Preheat the oven to 350°F (180°C). 2—Mince one of the onions and slice the other. In a large bowl, combine the beef, minced onions, garlic, and ¼ cup (60 mL) soy sauce. Generously season with black pepper and mix well to combine. 3—Grease a 6-cup (1.5 L) loaf pan. Press the meat mixture down into the pan, then cover with onion slices. 4—Set the loaf pan in a larger roasting pan. Pour boiling water into the roasting pan until it reaches midway up the loaf pan. Bake for 1 hour. 5—Serve the meatloaf hot, warm, or cold, with cucumber sticks, jasmine rice, and dipping bowls of soy sauce and bird's eye chili on the side.

BREAKFAST

One of my first school assignments in Quebec was to describe my breakfast. There were eight of us little Vietnamese children in the class, and we all repeated more or less the same words: "rice, pork, soup." When she saw our answers, our teacher, Marie-France, mimicked waking up—stretching, rubbing her eyes as she got out of bed—because she thought that we hadn't understood. It took a telephone conversation with my parents, who already spoke French, to translate not the words but the food traditions of the two cultures.

It's often said that to know what someone's mother tongue is, you should ask what language that person uses to count. For me, it's what I have for breakfast that shows I am not yet a *pure laine*, not yet 100 percent Québécoise, because even though I've lived in Quebec for forty years, I still don't eat cereal or toast. But neither do I enjoy a breakfast of a meal-in-a-bowl chicken soup, or rice with a piece of meatloaf and *bì* (shredded pork skin). As a result, I rarely eat in the morning. I think I've passed on that habit to my children, who refuse breakfast and often go to school on an empty stomach!

VIETNAMESE MEATLOAF
— THỊT CHƯNG TRỨNG

Serves 8 ✦ Prep time 30 minutes, including resting ✦ Cook time 1 hour

1 package (1.6 oz/45 g) mung bean vermicelli
  (glass noodles or angel hair)
1 lb (454 g) ground pork
1 cup (75 g) coarsely chopped mushrooms
½ cup (60 g) minced onions
2 whole eggs + 2 eggs, separated
¼ cup (60 mL) fish sauce

Sliced vegetables (e.g., cucumbers, radishes,
  green onions, daikon)
Fresh herbs (e.g.,basil, cilantro, Thai basil,
  Vietnamese coriander, mint)
1 batch green onion sauce (p. 24)
Dipping fish sauce (p. 23), for serving

1—Place the vermicelli in a large stainless-steel bowl, cover with cold water, and let rest for 15 minutes, stirring from time to time. 2—Preheat the oven to 350°F (180°C). 3—Drain the vermicelli thoroughly, then cut into 4-inch (10 cm) lengths and return to the bowl. 4—Add the ground pork, mushrooms, and onions. Using your hands, mix until the ingredients are thoroughly combined. 5—In a small bowl, whisk the two whole eggs with two egg whites (reserve the remaining yolks) and the fish sauce. Pour the egg mixture over the meat mixture and stir to combine. 6—Transfer the meat mixture to a 6-cup (1.5 L) greased loaf pan. Set the loaf pan in a larger roasting pan. Pour boiling water in the roasting pan until it reaches midway up the loaf pan. Bake for 1 hour. 7—Ten minutes before the end of the cooking time, brush the meatloaf with the remaining egg yolks and finish baking. 8—Spread the vegetables and herbs over a large serving dish. Slice the meatloaf and serve hot, warm, or cold, drizzled with green onion sauce and with small bowls of dipping fish sauce on the side.

Vietnamese meatloaf is often served for breakfast with rice, grilled pork chops, and some bì (p. 124).

Bì

Serves 2 ✦ Prep time 10 minutes ✦ Cook time 1 hour

1 lb (454 g) pork shoulder, rind on
Peanut oil, for cooking
4 cloves garlic, skin on
1 Tbsp (12 g) sugar

1 tsp (6 g) salt
⅓ cup (50 g) toasted rice flour
  (p. 27 or store-bought)
Freshly ground black pepper

1—Slice the pork in half. 2—Add a splash of oil to a stockpot set over medium heat. Add the garlic cloves and pork and cook without browning, turning the meat several times to coat with the oil. 3—Lower the heat to the minimum and keep cooking, uncovered, for 45 minutes, turning the meat several times along the way. By the end of the cooking time, the pork should be well done and the garlic flesh melting. 4—Transfer the meat to a cutting board and remove the rind, then thinly slice both the rind and the meat and transfer to a large stainless-steel bowl. Toss to combine. 5—Remove the skins from the garlic, then transfer to a small bowl and mash with a fork. Add the sugar, salt, toasted rice flour, and black pepper to taste, and stir to combine. Add the garlic mixture to the pork and toss to combine.

For a quick meal, serve some bì over cooked rice, garnished with green onion sauce (p. 24) and Vietnamese pickled vegetables (p. 31) and drizzled with two spoonfuls of dipping fish sauce (p. 23).

You can also stuff some bì into a baguette with fresh cilantro leaves to make a quick sandwich.

The freshest way to enjoy bì is to serve it over vermicelli and fresh herbs, drizzled with dipping fish sauce (p. 23). Add thinly sliced bird's eye chili to taste.

CARAMEL PORK STEW
— THỊT KHO

Serves 6 ✦ Prep time 20 minutes ✦ Cook time 2 hours 15 minutes

2¼ lb (1 kg) deboned pork shoulder,
   with or without rind

Peanut oil, for cooking

4 cloves garlic, minced

⅓ cup (73 g) brown sugar

13.5 oz (400 mL) coconut water

¼ cup (60 mL) fish sauce

1 Tbsp (15 mL) soy sauce

Freshly ground black pepper

6 hard-boiled eggs, peeled

Fresh cilantro leaves

1 batch bean sprout salad (p. 85), for serving

1—Slice the pork shoulder into large cubes. 2—Add a splash of oil to a stockpot set over medium-high heat, then brown the pork cubes on all sides. 3—Add the garlic and sauté for 1 minute. 4—Add the brown sugar and stir vigorously until a thick caramel forms. Remove from heat. 5—Add the coconut water (be careful, as the caramel may spatter), then incorporate the fish sauce and soy sauce. Generously season with black pepper and mix well. 6—Transfer back to the heat. Bring to a simmer, cover, and cook over low heat for 2 hours, stirring from time to time. 7—Twenty minutes before the end of the cooking time, add the whole hard-boiled eggs, making sure to coat them with the sauce. 8—Serve hot, garnished with cilantro leaves, with bean sprout salad on the side.

CHÀ BÔNG

During the years when the men were imprisoned in reeducation camps, the women would bring them this dried meat, which keeps for months. Eating just a pinch of it would give the impression of having eaten much more, because of the salty taste of the fish sauce. Otherwise, the men would have to be content with grasshoppers, ants, and their ration of one peanut per day. Now and then they were lucky enough to treat themselves to a festive meal if a foolhardy rat had ventured too close to those starving souls.

Today, I add *chà bông* to bowls of rice scented with a small knob of butter, or garnish a slice of buttered baguette with the meaty powder, and immediately a story gushes out—a tale arriving from a far-off land.

CHÀ BÔNG

Makes 2 cups (500 mL) ✦ Prep time 30 minutes ✦ Cook time 3 hours

2 lb (900 g) rindless pork loin
Freshly ground black pepper
⅓ cup (85 mL) fish sauce

2 Tbsp (25 g) sugar
2 cloves garlic, minced

1—Slice the pork loin into large cubes. Transfer the pork to a large stainless-steel bowl and generously season with black pepper. 2—Add the fish sauce, sugar, and garlic, and mix to combine. 3—Transfer the pork and flavorings to a stockpot. Set over medium heat, bring to a simmer, then lower the heat to the minimum, cover, and cook for 2 hours, stirring regularly. 4—Remove from heat and let cool. 5—Transfer the pork from the cooking liquid to a bowl, and shred the meat using two forks or a hand mixer. 6—Pour the cooking liquid over the shredded meat. Mix to combine, then transfer to a large skillet. 7—Cook over low heat, stirring regularly, until the liquid is almost completely evaporated. 8—From that point on, keep cooking, stirring regularly and rubbing the meat against the bottom of the pan to get a dry, woolly texture. This can take up to 45 minutes. 9—Let the meat cool completely and store in an airtight container. *Chà bông* will keep for up to a year at room temperature.

RICE PORRIDGE
— *CHÁO*

Serves 4 ✦ Cook time 2 hours

½ cup (93 g) jasmine rice   6 cups (1.5 L) water

1—In a stockpot over low heat, cook the rice and water together, stirring every so often until the mixture resembles oatmeal, about 2 hours. 2—Serve with *chà bông* (p. 130) or caramel pork (p. 67).

This rice porridge is the Vietnamese version of chicken noodle soup, purported to cure any malady, big or small! You should have some whenever you feel under the weather.

One night in Hanoi, a soup merchant located in front of my hotel made me some rice porridge topped with shredded shiso leaves to cure a fever. I felt better almost immediately. I'm still unsure whether it was the dish's healing power or the merchant's kindness that cured me.

BIG SISTER 2 — *LÝ THÀNH KIM THÚY*

My mother often tells me it was a good thing that she hadn't named me Thùy, with the grave accent over the u instead of the acute one, because thùy means delicacy and I am the very opposite.

I am infinitely impatient. I don't remember a time when I was able to wait until I got home before opening a box of pastries. I don't usually have any utensils in the car, so I'll stick my index finger right into the icing. If I find a parking ticket printed on heavy paper, I'll fold it in two and use it as a spoon. As for ice cream, I eat it directly from the container, biting anything that's near the edge and diligently licking the middle part. The next time you see an Asian woman on the road with her face in an ice-cream carton, you'll know it's me.

DESSERTS AND SNACKS

ICE CREAM

It's often said that the Vietnamese are quite willing to "Vietnamize" everything. Bánh mi came from France, as did *pâté de foie* and mayonnaise—but we add cilantro, marinated vegetables, and bits of fresh hot peppers. During my childhood, we ate our one and only cheese, *La vache qui rit*, along with a banana—and still do. Birthday cakes carried the powerful scent of durian. As for ice cream, the classic vanilla-chocolate-strawberry gave way to flavors like soursop, pandan leaves, or young rice.

When I was little, we knew that school would soon be over when we heard the bells of the ice-cream vendor calling to us on the sidewalk. He sold ice cream in cones or in small brioches. Even today, I like to savor my ice cream in a hamburger bun or a slice of soft bread. I guarantee that my version is tastier than any store-bought ice-cream sandwich.

FROZEN BANANAS
— *KEM CHUỐI*

Serves 8 ✦ Prep time 15 minutes + freezing

1 can (13.5 oz/400 mL) coconut cream

Pinch of salt

1 cup (50 g) sweetened coconut flakes

1 cup (120 g) crushed peanuts

8 ripe mini bananas

8 Chinese chopsticks

8 squares plastic wrap

1—Combine the coconut cream and salt in a shallow bowl. 2—Place the coconut flakes and crushed peanuts on two separate plates. 3—Peel the bananas and skewer onto the chopsticks. 4—Roll each banana in the coconut cream, then in the coconut flakes, and then in the peanuts. 5—Set each coated banana over a square of plastic wrap as you go, wrapping them tightly and gently pressing so the garnishes stick to the banana. 6—Freeze at least 4 hours before serving.

Sugarcane juice—the most refreshing of all!

FRIED BANANAS
— CHUỐI CHIÊN

Serves 4 ✦ Prep time 20 minutes, including resting ✦ Cook time 15 minutes

1½ cups (150 g) self-rising cake and
   pastry flour (Brodie or equivalent)
1½ Tbsp (14 g) rice flour
¼ cup (50 g) sugar

½ cup (125 mL) water + more if necessary
3 very ripe bananas
Vegetable oil, for frying

1—Combine the flours and the sugar in a stainless-steel bowl. Whisk in the water, then add more water as needed to create a thick crêpe-like batter. Let stand for 10 minutes.
2—Slice the bananas lengthwise into four pieces, then dip into the batter, making sure the bananas are fully coated. 3—In a large wok or a fryer, heat the oil to 325°F (160°C). Add the bananas, a few pieces at a time, and fry for about 5 minutes, until golden.
4—Transfer the fried bananas to a plate covered with paper towel. Serve hot.

CARAMEL FLAN
— BÁNH FLAN

Serves 6 ✦ Prep time 20 minutes + resting ✦ Cook time 45 minutes

1½ cups (300 g) sugar, divided
3 large eggs
2 Tbsp (30 mL) water

2 cups (500 mL) milk
1 tsp (5 mL) vanilla extract

1—Preheat the oven to 350°F (180°C). 2—In a small bowl, whisk half of the sugar with the eggs. 3—Combine the remaining sugar with the water in a small saucepan. Set over medium heat and cook, without stirring, until the mixture turns a deep amber caramel. 4—Divide the caramel between six ramekins and let cool. 5—In a small saucepan, heat the milk just to a simmer. Whisk the sugar and egg mixture into the milk, then divide between the ramekins. 6—Line a baking dish with a tea towel. Carefully transfer the ramekins to the prepared baking dish. Pour hot (not boiling) water into the baking dish until it reaches halfway up the ramekins. 7—Bake for 35 minutes. 8—Remove from the oven, then carefully lift the ramekins out of the hot water bath. Let the flans cool completely on the counter or in the refrigerator, at least 2 hours. 9—To serve, slide a sharp knife along the inside of the ramekins, then invert the flans onto serving plates.

You can place a thin slice of orange or mandarin in the bottom of each ramekin before pouring in the caramel.

Caramel flan is served all over Vietnam. It has graduated from being a French import to a Vietnamese dessert in its own right. I must admit that I think no other caramel flan compares with the Vietnamese version—but the ultimate flans are those made by my Aunt 8.

GUAVA

The day my father dared to stretch the budget to buy our first guava in Montreal, he seated all of the members of his little family around the table and served us each a tiny slice. He nearly held his breath as he watched us try it. He wanted to have us eat this new fruit from a place he had left and lost. He didn't dare hope that I'd have held in my memory the exact location of the guava tree in our Saigon courtyard. He didn't expect that my brothers would be able to recognize this fruit. And yet, guava became my brother Tin's favorite fruit, and to this day he likes it sprinkled with spiced salt, the Vietnamese way.

With Marike Paradis,
the artist whose vision
made this book possible.

SOURSOP SMOOTHIE
— SINH TỐ MẢNG CẦU

Serves 1 ◆ Prep time 5 minutes

1 cup (250 g) frozen soursop flesh

1 Tbsp (15 mL) sweetened condensed milk

Ice cubes

⅔ cup (170 mL) water

1—Add all ingredients to a blender and pulse until it reaches a smooth consistency. 2—Pour into a tall glass and serve.

If you can find fresh soursop, add 2 more tablespoons (30 mL) of sweetened condensed milk to the recipe.

VIETNAMESE TAPIOCA AND BANANA
— CHÈ CHUỐI

Serves 6 ✦ Prep time 5 minutes ✦ Cook time 15 minutes

2 cups (500 mL) water
Pinch of salt
¼ cup (38 g) dry tapioca pearls
3 Tbsp (36 g) sugar
1 cup (250 mL) coconut milk

⅓ cup (40 g) crushed peanuts
1 Tbsp (9 g) toasted sesame seeds
2 very ripe bananas, peeled and cut into
   thick slices.

1—In a saucepan, bring the water to a boil. Add the salt and tapioca pearls, then lower the heat and simmer, stirring regularly, until the pearls are translucent. Remove from heat. 2—Stir in the sugar and coconut milk and mix well. 3—In a small bowl, combine the peanuts and sesame seeds. Set aside. 4—Upon serving, stir banana slices into the warm tapioca, divide into dishes, and garnish with the peanut and sesame mixture.

My father was crazy about automobiles. Had he been born in another time and another place he'd have been a collector. Now though, with a war being fought, it was unseemly to park his car in a schoolyard only to find it at the end of the day covered with the flame red petals of the flamboyant tree. It was indecent to drive for two hours, to cover thirty-seven kilometers on a dirt road scattered with crevices from exploded mines, to have a coffee with his grandfather, even if the coffee they served was a rare one, made from beans eaten by foxes but not digested. According to coffee enthusiasts a single cup of that brew would be intoxicating because the beans underwent a fermentation process in the foxes' stomachs before they followed nature's usual course.

Today, my father still thinks that the coffee sent to him from Vietnam is the best. He prepares it every morning, placing a spoonful in a filter that he sets directly onto the glass. He pours the hot water into it and watches the drops fall, one by one, onto the layer of condensed milk in the bottom. Plop . . . plop . . . plop . . . Maybe someday I'll suggest that he come away with me, travel the old route, to share a "fox scat coffee" and see the wind in his hair that is now gray like his grandfather's.

—from *À Toi*, by Kim Thúy and Pascal Janovjak (Libre Expression, 2011)

NATHALIE'S MATCHA TEA COOKIES

Makes about 48 cookies ✤ Prep time 20 minutes + 2 hours resting ✤ Cook time
9 to 12 minutes

2 cups (250 g) all-purpose flour

1 tsp (5 g) baking powder

½ tsp (2 g) baking soda

2 Tbsp (6 g) matcha tea powder

⅔ cup (150 g) salted butter, softened

1 cup (220 g) brown sugar

2 eggs

½ cup (70 g) toasted pine nuts

7 oz (200 g) white chocolate, chopped

Wax paper or plastic wrap

1—Sift the flour, baking powder, baking soda, and matcha tea powder together. Set aside.
2—Cream the butter using a hand mixer or a stand mixer. 3—Add the brown sugar and beat
until the mixture is light and fluffy. 4—Add the eggs and beat to combine. 5—Mix in the
flour mixture in three batches, beating well after each addition. 6—Add the pine nuts and
chocolate and stir just to incorporate. 7—Divide the dough into four portions and set each
portion on a piece of wax paper or plastic wrap. 8—Shape the dough into 2-inch (5 cm)
diameter rolls. Wrap well in the wax paper or plastic wrap, twisting both ends to seal shut.
9—Refrigerate for at least 2 hours. 10—Preheat the oven to 325°F (160°C). 11—Slice each
roll into 10 to 12 cookies. Place the cookies on parchment paper–lined baking sheets.
Bake for 9 to 12 minutes, depending on whether you like a softer cookie or a crisper one.

Using sushi mats to shape the dough into rolls will enable you to create
perfectly round cookies.

The cookie rolls will keep refrigerated for up to 1 week, or frozen for up
to 6 months. Thaw the rolls in the refrigerator for 24 hours before slicing.

With Michelle Bouffard.

VIETNAMESE FOOD–WINE PAIRINGS

MICHELLE BOUFFARD, SOMMELIER

It is said that for the Vietnamese, food is the messenger of love. The generosity expressed by an overabundance of delights on the table is a sign of affection.

Kim's car is like a cafeteria. For a trip between two destinations, no matter how brief, it's rare that she doesn't offer a smoothie, a cookie, or a pastry to her passenger. She becomes obsessed with delivering homemade soup if someone she loves has come down with a virus. And even if I tell her in advance what I'm serving when I invite her to eat at my place, she brings an entire meal.

Kim prefers the hardwood floor to the sofa for after-dinner conversations. Serious discussions, though, take place in the doorway at the end of the evening. She doesn't drink alcohol, which is just as well, because evening parties would last until daybreak. We stand around, with or without coats on, hands empty or full, as goodbyes are transformed into philosophical discussions that end in the wee hours. When she is surrounded by people she cares about, time stops. Actions speak louder than words, even for a writer.

RIESLING

I've always thought that a country's food and a region's wine are like journals. They bear within them the history of a land, the preoccupations of a moment, and the emotions of the present. Every bite, every sip reveals secrets to anyone who takes the trouble to listen.

Two of my best friends are Vietnamese. Even though I've never set foot on their native soil, I have only to close my eyes and think about the flavors of their cuisine and I'll feel as if I am really there. The aromas of the various dishes form a symbiosis between coolness that revives and sugar that induces sleepiness.

The powerful ingredients of Vietnamese cuisine require a wine with a strength of character to match them. Riesling is the ideal candidate. Always direct and decisively acid with pronounced aromatic flavors, it exudes freshness. Don't be misled by its exuberant notes, which waver between citrus and stone fruits; its body is much lighter than you might expect. Chameleon-like, it can be dry but also slightly sweet, even very sweet; it's up to the winemaker. If there is residual sugar, it gives the illusion that the wine's acidity is lower than it is.

I prefer a slightly sweet Riesling to harmonize with the ever-present sugar in Vietnamese recipes. The delicacy of German Rieslings makes them highly recommendable, but Canada, the Alsace region of France, Austria, and Australia also offer some fine choices. To serve with desserts, choose from the sweetest options.

It's said of Riesling that it is a noble variety of grape. When it travels, it maintains its strength of character, its individuality. It shines in cooler climates and manages to survive even the rigors of winter. Its cheerful nature and its lightness make one forget its forthright complexity. Graced with good genes, it evokes grandeur while still young, but as it ages, time makes it even greater, with its mineral tones becoming apparent.

The path of a life is drawn by the choices we make. I could have brought up wines such as Albariño, Gewürztraminer, Assyrtiko, Pinot Blanc, and many others. But what I want to tell you is the story of a young girl who fled with her family across the terrors of the ocean to end up here with us. The warrior possesses the qualities of Riesling. She continues to sow hope and to light candles despite the intensity of her past.

TO DRINK . . .

Nothing is ever black or white. But there are progressions. We can always count on the aromatic range of Riesling to awaken our taste buds and on its backbone to call us to order. Resisting its temptation is impossible. To explore the nuances of its character, the names of a few good wineries follow.

Riesling may be served with the meal or the dessert. The following suggestions are for table wines, but there are sweet elixirs to accompany dessert that are also worth trying.

GERMANY

The Germans reserve the throne for Riesling. Its characteristics vary from region to region, but in general, it is marked by a light body and a fairly low alcohol level. A number of table wines have a hint of residual sugar to balance the high acidity, but those who prefer a dry Riesling can also find some impressive bottles. I am particularly fond of the ones from the Mosel region: Rheingau, Rhine-Hesse, Nahe, and Pfalz.

FAVORITE WINERIES: Dr. Loosen, Dönnhoff, Joh. Jos. Prüm, Keller, Künstler, Selbach Oster, Emrich-Schönleber, Schäfer-Fröhlich, Gunderloch.

ALSACE

Rieslings from the Alsace region of France have more body and a higher alcohol content than the German Rieslings. Table wines may be dry or slightly sweet, depending on the producer.

FAVORITE WINERIES: Domaine Albert Mann, Domaine Barmès-Buecher, Josmeyer, Domaine Weinbach, Domaine Ostertag, Domaine Marcel Deiss, Domaine Zind-Humbrecht.

AUSTRIA

Neither light nor heavy, Austrian Rieslings are nearly always dry and often austere when young. While Riesling is not the king of the region's grape varieties, its grandeur and its elegance are quite wonderful. Those from the regions of Kamptal, Kremstal, and Wachau are particularly impressive.

FAVORITE WINERIES: Bernhard Ott, Alzinger, FX Pichler, Hirsch, Geyerhof, Loimer, Pichler-Krutzler.

AUSTRALIA

The regions of Clare Valley and Eden Valley are synonymous with dry and moderately full-bodied Rieslings. The juicy flavors of stone fruits and red grapefruit are readily detectable. Some, however, such as those from Grosset, need a few years in the cellar before opening.

FAVORITE WINERIES: Pewsey Vale, Grosset.

CANADA

For the modern wine lover, British Columbia and Ontario make some impressive Rieslings. Ontario and B.C. producers generally follow the style of one of the four traditional Riesling regions mentioned above.

FAVORITE WINERIES: Little Farm, Tantalus, Cave Spring, Mission Hill Family Estate, 13th Street, Cedar Creek Estate, Orofino.

VIETNAMESE FOOD–MUSIC PAIRINGS

Selected with love by radio personality
Monique Giroux, inspired by Kim Thúy.

C'EST BEAU LA VIE ✦ Catherine Deneuve and Benjamin Biolay

CE JOUR-LÀ SUR LE MÉKONG ✦ Gabriel Yared

CRÈME GLACÉE ✦ Tristan Malavoy

ÉCRIVAINE ✦ Dumas

HANOI ✦ La grande Sophie

HANOI CAFÉ ✦ Bleu Toucan

HANOI CAFÉ, INSTRUMENTAL ✦ Ron Korb

IL Y AVAIT UN JARDIN ✦ Georges Moustaki

LA JOIE DE VIVRE ✦ Monique Leyrac

LE PETIT PAIN AU CHOCOLAT ✦ Joe Dassin

LES COOKIES DE KIM ✦ Véronique Merveille

LES Z'HERBES ✦ Anne Sylvestre

MON PAYS ✦ Gilles Vigneault

NOS MOTS ✦ Luciole

OVER THE RAINBOW ✦ Israel Kamakawiwo'ole

TENIR DEBOUT ✦ David Portelance

TU ✦ Umberto Tozzi

UN GELATO AL LIMON ✦ Paolo Conte

UNE GLACE AU SOLEIL ✦ Gaby Laplante

VIENNE L'AMOUR ✦ Fred Pellerin

ACKNOWLEDGEMENTS

There are a number of us responsible for this book,
each playing a specific role.

Me, I tell stories.

NATHALIE BÉLAND wrote the recipes with the proper quantities, the proper proportions, and the proper cooking time, in spite of my attempts to lead her astray with my imaginary measurements: "It's instant cooking, you wash your hands and it's done." "You cut the green onion in three." "You take it off the heat when it's yellow like the sand of the Magdalen Islands." Her patience is boundless, with me at any rate. Most of all, her efficiency transformed this painstaking work into a culinary journey that was both amusing and enlightening.

ÉRIC RÉGIMBALD is the man who caramelized the pieces of pork one by one with a surgeon's tweezers. Don't say it too loudly, but his caramelized pork was almost better than my mother's.

SARAH SCOTT is the one who perched on the edge of my desk, on tiptoe, to take photos of stems of cilantro and basil that went limp every sixty seconds. I kept taking pictures of Sarah while her own camera went on clicking. She is beautiful from every angle. In a thousand ways, she could make a grilled eggplant come alive, make even a piece of tofu attractive. Then she won me over totally with her affectionate and sensitive way of looking at my many mothers: Big Sister 3 and my aunts.

Along with Sarah were three other photographers: GILLES DUFOUR saw Vietnam with a lover's eyes. He immortalized it in images with the same love and wonder as I feel. TRI became my little brother when I arrived in Hanoi alone and confused in a country I barely knew. His photos haunted me then and haunt me still. QUÔC captured the beauty of my grandmother, his great-grandmother, very shortly before her final breath. She posed for him, for his school project, in the silence and complicity of two individuals who love one another unconditionally.

Between MARIKE PARADIS and me it was love at first sight when we met to discuss the cover of my first novel, *Ru*. My affection and admiration for her grow stronger year by year, project by project. Without Marike I wouldn't have had the courage or the ability necessary to create a book of recipes. Marike sees what I'm unable to illustrate in words; she hears my breath behind my thoughts. She reads my fingers even when they're motionless. She always finds the color, the tone, the rhythm that reveal precisely the impalpable universe I want to share with you. Marike is a good fairy who makes my dreams come true before I even know enough to conceive them. There are a dozen years—and a dozen inches—between Marike and me, yet I have the impression that we're twins when together we leaf through books in a peaceful corner of a bookstore. Our shared pleasure in cooperation has given birth to this book that immortalizes the delicacy of the signature and the strength of Marike's talent.

April 6, 1923 – January 1, 2016

MATERNAL GRANDMOTHER — *LÊ KIÊM GƯƠNG*

She had eight living children, two boys and six girls.
A month before her death, we were four generations
streaming around her hospital bed.

Until the very last second, she knew all our names as well as where we lived, what we did, our successes—even those of the youngest ones. She was particularly concerned about our love lives! She could see the sorrow behind our smiles. She listened to us express our fears, our giddiness. She was our queen, a queen admired by all her descendants. At each of our graduations, even the one from kindergarten, she could never stop referring to the death of her husband: "Poor man, he didn't share my luck at living long enough for all this joy."

I dare to confess that I was her favorite among her seventeen grandchildren, two great-grandchildren, and one great-great-granddaughter. She liked to tell people that I was proof that what is inside a person affects the outside, that we could become physically beautiful without plastic surgery!

My grandmother paid us compliments straightforwardly, unreservedly. Her greatest talent was to make each of us think that we were her favorite. She loved us all purely and unconditionally regardless of our wrongs and weaknesses. In return we all loved her blindly and we love her still. For between her and us there had been Life. What is left today is Love.

INDEX

180

There are lots of men in my life too.
One day I'll talk to you about them, I promise.